God Magnified, Part 9

Abiding in the Lord of Hosts

I0191579

By Eric Mumford

LIFECHANGERS®

P.O. Box 3709 ❖ Cookeville, TN 38502
931.520.3730 ❖ lc@lifechangers.org

The Scripture quotations contained in this book are from:

The New American Standard Bible®, Copyright © 1960, 1962, 1963, 1971, 1972, 1973, 1975, 1977, 1995 by The Lockman Foundation. *The Amplified Bible.* 1987. La Habra, CA: The Lockman Foundation.

PLUMBLINE

Published by:

P.O. Box 3709 | Cookeville, TN 38502
(800) 521-5676 | www.lifechangers.org

All Rights Reserved
ISBN 978-1-940054-08-7

Contents

God Magnified Statements
15 Pillars of the Trinity's Dwelling Place

Pillar 1 | God is an "**Us**"– three Individuals (Gen. 1:26, 3:22, 11:7; Isa. 6:8).

Pillar 2 | "God is **One**" (Deut. 6:4; Mark 12:29).

Pillar 3 | "God is **Love (*Agape*)**" (1 John 4:8, 16).

Pillar 4 | "God is a **sun**" (Psa. 84:11).

Pillar 5 | "**Holy, Holy, Holy** is the Lord God, the Almighty" (Rev. 4:8; Isa. 6:3).

Pillar 6 | "God is **Light**" (1 John 1:5).

Pillar 7 | "The eternal God is a **dwelling place**" (Deut. 33:27).

Pillar 8 | "God **in Christ**" (Col. 2:9; 2 Cor. 5:19; Eph. 4:32).

Pillar 9 | "God is **spirit**" (John 4:24).

Pillar 10 | "God is **true**" (John 3:33).

Pillar 11 | "God Most High" (Ps. 78:35; Heb. 7:1).

Pillar 12 | "The Lord is a God of **justice**" (Isa. 30:18).

Pillar 13 | "The Lord, whose name is *Jealous*, is a **jealous** God" (Ex. 34:14).

Pillar 14 | "God is a **consuming fire**" (Deut. 4:24; Heb. 12:29).

Pillar 15 | God is three sacrificial **Self-sharers** (Eph. 4:7-10).

God Magnified, Part 9

Abiding in the Lord of Hosts

By Eric Mumford

The *God is* statements of the Scriptures are like pillars of a covered porch built around the entire circumference of **God is a dwelling place**; each pillar serves as a lens to see and understand the next. Progressive magnification of these *God is* declarations leads to a three-dimensional understanding of the eternal kingdom and draws us to enter and participate as *sharers* through the God-Man Jesus in the eternal life of Father, Son, and Spirit—our Triune-God. As kingdom emigrants, we are pioneering forward together into this unfolding revelation of **the fusion of the Trinity**.

In the previous volume, *God Magnified Part 8: Unveiling Three Sacrificial Self-sharers*, we learned that mature *Agape* is reciprocal self-sharing Love. We discovered through the Scriptures that Father, Son, and Spirit *share* all things with One Another; and that all the fullness of these things were *shared* with the Son Jesus as a Man; and how, in this God-Man, the Triune-God *share* all things with us human beings who have bought into Him by faith: "**All things belong to you,** and **you belong to Christ;** and **Christ belongs to God**" (1 Cor. 3:22-23).

The kingdom of God is a cohabitation of self-sharers; Father, Son, and Spirit steward this **one shared estate** on behalf of One Another and on our behalf as "heirs of God and fellow heirs with Christ" (Rom. 8:17). Paul wrote: "That you will know how one [*individual*] ought to conduct himself in the household [*cohabitation*] of God, which is the church of the living God [*three Self-sharers*], **the pillar and support of the truth** [*Triune-Agape*]" (1 Tim. 3:15).

In this volume, *God Magnified Part 9: Abiding in the Lord of Hosts,* we will see that Father, Son, and Spirit are profoundly inclusive and hospitable. Through the Spirit, the Son Jesus prayed to Father for you and me, saying, "**That they also may be in Us**…that they may be one, just as We are one" (John 17:21-22). These three, eternal Self-sharers have purposed to include you and me in Their own relational fusion and inter-personal oneness known as the kingdom of God. As a Host, the Trinity have invited *hosts* of unique individuals to cohabit with Them in the combined and combining God-Man Jesus Christ who embodies within Himself this shared kingdom.

The Scriptures illustrate the blueprints of this relational, inter-personal infrastructure in various and creative ways. In this *Plumbline*, we will examine these blueprints **from macro to micro**: 1. individual **stars** encompass the nucleus of one galaxy and move together in the swirling arms of this vortex; 2. individual, unlocked **gardens** adjoin one another and become one shared estate; 3. **living stones** are fit together on one Cornerstone and become one building; 4. individual **members** are incorporated into the one body (corpus) of one Man, Christ Jesus.

The Lord God of Hosts

Our Triune-God is called the **"Lord God of hosts"** (Ps. 89:8) in the Scriptures more than 280 times! Jeremiah affirmed, "For the Maker of all is He, and Israel is the tribe of His inheritance; **the Lord of hosts is His name**" (Jer. 10:16). In hospitality, a *host* invites a group of people—*hosts* of individuals or groups of individuals—into his own home. A *host* extends an invitation to these *hosts* of unique, diverse persons because he desires to strengthen his relationship with each of them and, as a sharer and servant, he desires to facilitate an environment in which these individuals may build relationships with one another.

The God-Man Jesus is the **bodily Home** (corpus, Nucleus) in Whom Father, Son, and Spirit cohabit with One Another in fusion Oneness: "For in Him all the fullness of Deity **dwells in bodily form**, and in Him you have been made full" (Col. 2:9-10). Into this God-Man Nucleus, multitudes of unique, individual human beings have been invited not merely as visitors but to **dwell** permanently *with* these three Self-sharers and **abide** eternally *in* Them. Within the bodily Nucleus of Christ, the Triune-God as our *Host* also desire that we, as *hosts* of individuals, families, tribes, and nations, cohabit together in *Agape*—reciprocal *gene-rosity* and sacrificial self-sharing equality—according to Their own image and likeness.

The master-key verse that opens and defines the ultimate kingdom purpose of the Lord God of hosts is Jesus' prayer in John 17:

> [21]That they [*individual believers*] may all be one; even as You, Father, are in Me and I in You, **that they also may be in Us** [*sharers in Our fusion oneness*], so that the world may believe that You sent Me [*to be the God-Man Nucleus, to embody the cohabitation of the Trinity and man: the kingdom*]. [22]The glory [*fuse-able DNA of Agape*] which You have given Me [*as a Man*] I have given to them [*made communicable in a new, gene-rous bloodline*], **that they may be one, just as We** [*Father, Son, Spirit*] **are one**; [23]I in them and You in Me, that they may be **perfected in unity** [*sacrificial self-sharers in Trinity-like fusion*], so that the world may know that You sent Me, and loved them, even as You have loved Me [*so all the myriad hosts of mankind may receive Our invitation and join those We are already hosting*].

> [24]Father, I desire that they also, whom You have given Me, **be with Me where I am** [*incorporated into My corpus*], so that

they may see My glory which You have given Me [*as the God-Man Nucleus*], for You loved Me before the foundation of the world. ^{25}O righteous Father, although the world has not known You, yet I have known [*cohabited with*] You; and these have known that You sent Me; ^{26}and I have made Your name known to them, and will make it known, so **that the love** [*lit. Agape*] **with which You loved Me may be in them** [*e.g. re-gene-ration*], and I in them (John 17:21-26).

As sacrificial Self-sharers, the deepest heart-cry of Father, Son, and Spirit is that you "may be in Us" (vs. 21). Hearing and understanding this eternal desire of **inclusive hospitality** helps us to see and know our Triune-God as **the Lord of hosts**. Fulfilling God's desire by **relocating** into the God-Man Nucleus and abiding in fusion oneness with the Trinity and one another in Him is the deepest and truest form of worth-ship you or I can offer because it is **the fulfillment of the purpose of our very existence**.

Stars in the Arms of One Galaxy

In the *natural* creation, the pattern and structure of a **galaxy** intentionally illustrates this relational, inter-personal infrastructure of *hosts* of individuals encompassing the Nucleus of God in Christ. David recognized the *spiritual* pattern of the kingdom: "**Let the assembly of the peoples** [*myriads of individuals*] **encompass You** [*as the epicenter of their cohabitation*], and over them return on high [*God Most High: three Who exalt One Another*]" (Ps. 7:7). A galaxy is a **fusion vortex** that moves in the pattern of a **whirlwind**: "In whirlwind and storm is His way" (Nah. 1:3). The center of a galaxy, called the nucleus, is a **stellar nursery**—a fusion epicenter that gives birth to new stars which encompass (surround) the nucleus in its swirling arms: "The eternal God [*three sacrificial Self-sharers*] is a dwelling place, and **underneath are the everlasting arms**" (Deut. 33:27).

The Son Jesus taught us to pray, "Our Father who is in heaven…Your **kingdom** [*cohabitation*] come. Your will be done, **on earth as it in heaven**" (Matt. 6:9-10). In heaven, angels, other living creatures, and human beings who have passed through death into that realm, all move together in the everlasting arms of the eternal vortex of the Trinity. All individual stars, which were born out of the perpetual fusion of Father, Son, and Spirit, **move together in one, life-giving direction with their Triune-Creator**—the "Us" of our genesis (Gen. 1:26).

Human beings who are re-gene-rating in *Agape* by faith and reciprocal gene-rosity are referred to in the Scriptures as **the stars of God** (see Gen. 26:4; Deut. 1:10; Isa. 14:13; Dan. 12:3; Matt. 13:43). However, you and I cannot be stars autonomously, that is, apart from the Nucleus. God said of the archangel Lucifer,

"How you have fallen from heaven, O the **star** of the morning, son of the dawn [*created out of the fusion of the Trinity*]!" (Isa. 14:12). When Lucifer bought into his own lie of *eros* individualism and attempted to be an **autonomous star**, he fell out of the Triune-Vortex, imploded, and became a **black hole**—an inverted, life-taking vortex: "His tail swept away a third of **the stars of heaven** [*angels who followed him*] and threw them to the earth" (Rev. 12:4). Further, when human beings bought into "the father of the lie" (John 8:44) we *fell* with him and became "**wandering stars**" (Jude 1:13) who willfully depart from the path of our intended orbit around the Nucleus of the galaxy. This ongoing saga is the original *Star Wars*!

The sign of Christ's birth was a "**star**" (Matt. 2:9) indicating that the God-Man Nucleus of the fusion of the Trinity and mankind had entered as "Savior" among the captives of Worthless' world of individualism, relational fission, con-fusion, and darkness. To follow the Man Jesus in His death and resurrection means we are *re-gene-rating* as stars who learn to move as one with "Jesus...**the bright morning star**" (Rev. 22:16) as sacrificial self-sharers in the eternal, life-giving Vortex of the Trinity. Some stars are larger and brighter than others, "for star differs from star in glory" (1 Cor. 15:41), but all share the same Source, **all are sharers in the one celestial body of God in Christ**, all are fueled in the same way, and all move together in the same direction in the everlasting arms.

This is the fulfillment of God's promise to Abraham: "I will multiply your descendants as **the stars of heaven**...and by your descendants [*self-sharers*] all the nations of the earth shall be blessed" (Gen. 26:4). As believers, you and I are "the children of the promise" (Rom. 9:8). As our father and forerunner, Abraham emigrated into these everlasting arms by "faith working through *Agape*" (Gal. 5:6). God also revealed these *hosts* of stars to Isaiah:

> ²²It is He who sits above the circle of the earth [*God Most High: Three humble Eternals mutually exalting One Another in downward ascent*], and its inhabitants are like grasshoppers [*e.g. dirt-dwellers*]; Who stretches out **the heavens like...a tent to dwell in** [*inclusive hospitality*]. ²³He it is who **reduces rulers to nothing** [*upward descent*], Who makes the **judges** of the earth **meaningless** [*overrules unjust authority*]. ²⁴Scarcely have they been planted, scarcely have they been **sown** [*e.g. dirt-bags filled with Worthless' de-gene-rate seed*], scarcely has their stock [*toxic influence*] taken **root** in the earth, but He merely blows on them, and they **wither** [*fission decay*], and the storm [*Triune-Vortex*] carries them away like stubble.

[25]"To whom [*e.g. to what corrupt individualist*] then will you liken Me [*three sacrificial Self-sharers*] that I would be **his equal**?" says the Holy One [*Holy, Holy, Holy: three Self-less Eternals in fusion Oneness*]. [26]Lift up your eyes on high and see who has created these **stars** [*light-bearing vortices of fusion; type of God's re-gene-rating children*], the One [*Three-in-One*] who **leads forth their host by number**, He calls them all by name; because of the greatness of His might [*All-Three-Mighty*] and the strength of His [*fusion*] power, **not one of them is missing** [*each individual is jealously cherished*] (Isa. 40:22-26).

Buying a Share in One Shared Estate

As one Triune-God, Father, Son, and Spirit *share* one nature, one Nucleus, one name, one purpose, one inheritance, and one estate—a cohabitation known as **the kingdom of God**. As the Lord God of hosts, these three Self-sharers desire to *share* with us the inheritance of this one estate. Our Triune-God does not have an inheritance to give you and me as individual proprietors; the only inheritance Father, Son, and Spirit have to give is offering us **a share** in Their one shared estate. Sacrificial self-sharing (*Agape*) is the sole means of true, abundant, eternal life because

in the Us of our genesis there is no inheritance for me, only an inheritance for us.

The archangel Lucifer *fell* because he bought into his own lie of *self-worth-ship;* he **refused to share**, and he *de-gene-rated* into "Belial [*lit. Worthless*]" (2 Cor. 6:15). The possessiveness and ownership into which all of us have been acculturated in Worthless' world effectively *short-circuits* the relational dynamic of *sharing* the kingdom. Me and mine will *eclipse, displace,* and *scatter* ours—*our* inheritance.

All human beings have a common origin: "The rich and the poor have **a common bond,** the Lord [*the Us: three Self-sharers*] is the maker of them all" (Prov. 22:2). All believers share "**a common faith**" (Titus 1:4). The fusion of individual believers *together* in the Nucleus of Christ is "**our common salvation**" (Jude 3). Paul wrote, "But to each one [*individual*] is given the manifestation [*gifts*] of the Spirit for **the common good**" (1 Cor. 12:7). "*Agape* **feasts**" (Jude 12) are *corporate* feasts in which individual believers come together to share, eat, and assimilate Jesus' flesh and blood—three Ingredients mixed and baked by *Agape* into **One Cake**. As individuals *share* this One Cake in faith and reciprocal faith-fullness, *together* they are assimilated as members into His **one body**.

Look at the first church: "And the congregation of those who believed were of **one heart and soul** [*Trinity-like*]; and not one [*individual*] of them claimed that anything belonging to him was his own [*proprietorship*], but all things were **common property** to them [*one shared estate*]" (Acts 4:32). It is evident that a community that actively *shares* one faith, one meal, gifts from one Spirit, and material possessions would require **cruciformity**—*gen-uine* **sacrificial self-sharing** from each individual on a daily basis! In the kingdom of our Triune-God, there is no **proprietorship**; in this one shared estate, there is only **stewardship**. "A servant who acts wisely [*as a Trinity-like steward*] will rule over a son who acts shamefully [*as a self-indulgent opportunist*], and will **share in the inheritance among brothers**" (Prov. 17:2).

In Jesus' parable of the prodigal, the younger of the two sons said to his father, " '**Father, give me the share of the estate which falls to me**.' So he **divided** his wealth between them [*fission*]" (Luke 15:12). As an individualist, the prodigal desired to pursue the mirage of **self-indulgence** "on a journey into a distant country" (Luke 15:13). This is relational fission: "He who separates himself seeks his own desire" (Prov. 18:1). In **self-worth-ship**, the son *devalued* and *disowned* his father, his brother, and the estate they shared with him. According to Worthless' world economics, he *debited* their one shared estate to *credit* himself. Knowing his father was a sacrificially *gene-rous* man, the son calculated his father would grant his share of the wealth to him. Jesus exposed *eros* calculation: "**Is your eye envious because I am gene-rous?**" (Matt. 20:15).

The father knew his son could never become a **true self-sharer in the bounty of their one shared**

estate until he came to the end of himself among other **opportunists in the famine of Worthless' world**; therefore, the father had no choice but to give his son over to his own desire (see Ps. 81:12; Rom. 1:24f). The father's foremost desire was for his two sons to *share* one family estate—to mature as sacrificial self-sharers who would **recognize one another as their true inheritance and cherish that oneness** rather than their own current net worth of material assets (mammon), immediate gratification, or future income potential. Paul became a sharer in the Trinity's economy of worth:

> **My beloved brothers** [*re-gene-rating in one new bloodline*], **whom I long to see** [*magnetism of reciprocal Agape*] **my joy and crown** [*in kingdom economics our treasure and inheritance is one another*] **in this way** [*fusion Oneness by sacrificial self-sharing*] **stand firm in the Lord** [*abide together in Christ, the Nucleus of the Trinity*], **my beloved** (Phil. 4:1).

Shareholders

The economy of Worthless' world operates largely upon international stock markets where exchanges take place. **Individuals buy shares in corporations** (equitable portions of a company's assets) providing capital for the business to grow and make a profit.

The term *corporation* comes from **corpus** meaning a body. Individuals design, develop, and legally register a corporation and invite others to buy into it as **shareholders**. Because this organization is a *corpus* with a legal identity of its own apart from its creators or investors, it may be sued in a court of law just like an individual human being. See Noah Webster's definition:

> **Corporate**, a. Latin, *corporatus*, to be shaped into a body, from *corpus*, body. United in a body, or community, as a number of individuals, who are empowered to transact business as an individual; formed into a body…United, general, collectively one.

> **Corporation**, n. A body politic or corporate, formed and authorized by law to act as a single person; a society having the capacity of transacting business as an individual. Corporations are aggregate [*e.g. shareholders*] or sole [*e.g. a solitary owner; no shares*]. Corporations aggregate consist of two or more persons united in a society, which is preserved either forever, or till the corporation is dissolved by the power that formed it (*American Dictionary of the English Language*, Noah Webster, 1828).

Individual shareholders (investors) certainly *share* a concern for the welfare of an aggregate corporation but only insofar as each individual can profit from owning these shares or by selling them at an opportune time for **personal advantage**—to amass personal wealth the individual is not required to share. Since each investor ultimately counts his own personal interests far dearer than the welfare of the corporation, these are systems of **con-fusion** and **reciprocal usury**. Beneath the veneer of these markets and companies, we often find varying degrees of fraud, embezzlement, insider trading, improper use of designated funds, and the exploitation of its employees.

The eternal kingdom is also a *corporation* of sorts—a bountiful, **fruit-bearing estate,** which Father, Son, and Spirit *are* and *share* in reciprocal *gene-rosity*. This family estate is uncreated, unshakable, and has no end because the **three Shareholders**—*"the incorruptible God"* (Rom. 1:23)—will not sell Their share for personal advantage under any circumstances like the prodigal son who sold his father, his brother, and their shared estate. Further, the kingdom is a **non-profit corporation**—Father, Son, and Spirit do not hoard Their gene-rous bounty to spend on Themselves. In Christ, They have extravagantly poured out all the fullness of its profits upon Their unworthy creation as the cost of our **redemption** (see 1 Pet. 1:18-20).

These three Shareholders made Their own private, family business a public corporation, or ***corpus***, into which other individuals may invest themselves and become shareholders. Father and Spirit invested all the fullness of Themselves into the Son—into the human body of the God-Man Jesus Christ—and made Him **the uncreated corpus** (body) **of this shared estate** (corporation) so that human beings could buy into Him (God in Christ) as self-sharers: "Now **you are Christ's body** [*incorporated into the corpus*] **and individually members of it** [*the kingdom corporation: cohabitation*]" (1 Cor. 12:27). Human beings buy into the one shared estate in the *corpus* of Christ at the cost of "losing" their own autonomous lives: "**All things belong to you** [*"fellow heirs (shareholders) with Christ"*], **and you belong to Christ** [*the corpus: the God-Man Nucleus*]; **and Christ belongs to God** [*the Nucleus of the Oneness (corporation) of the Trinity*]" (1 Cor. 3:22).

As shareholders, human beings are **adopted as legal heirs** and progressively **naturalized** (*re-generated*) **as self-sharers** who come to cherish this one shared estate with God and one another far dearer than their own lives! Paul testified, "I do not consider my life of any account as dear to myself" (Acts 20:24), and "I will most gladly **spend and be expended for your souls**" (2 Cor. 12:15). As an individual shareholder, I must learn how to willingly and repeatedly sustain personal losses for the sake of the whole, "**knowing that whatever** good [*sacrificial*] thing each one does [*for the corpus*], this he will **receive back from the Lord** [*three Self-sharers*]" (Eph. 6:8).

Most Christians have some understanding that **the church is "the body of Christ"** (Eph. 4:12). Yet, many of us believers approach this *corpus* in the same way an individualist relates to a *corporation* in Worthless' world—beneath the pretense of concern for the whole body lies **self-interest**. I become a shareholder in Christ's many-membered body based on **calculations** of what that *corporation* can do for me and not what I can do for His other members as a self-sharer, and I will only continue to invest in His church as long it benefits me. To love Jesus for His own sake, to truly serve Him and God in Him, means sacrificially sharing self with the members of His Own body. If we are unwilling to do this, "expecting nothing in return" (Luke 6:35), we are religious **mercenaries**.

Paul warned, "Now this I say, he [*the individualist*] who sows sparingly will also reap sparingly [*famine*] and he [*the self-sharer*] who sows bountifully will also reap bountifully" (2 Cor. 9:6). When I come among the members of Christ's church for *self-interest* rather than coming as a sacrificial *self-sharer* ready and willing to practice *reciprocal gene-rosity*, **my incorporation into Christ's body is artificial**, or at best **superficial**, and therefore, fruitless and futile. Consider these examples:

I am weak; I need strength to continue living my life therefore I come seeking the worship experience that will edify me, the individualist. I *use* Christ and His Father, His Spirit, and the other members within Him to recharge me. After a while I say, "This church just doesn't feed me anymore," and I sell. **I am lonely;** therefore, I come seeking like-minded friends, but as an individualist, I inadvertently drain them, they become a liability to me interfering with the attainment of my own desire. Soon I say, "This church just doesn't add to me," and I sell. **I am self-condemned;** I come to alleviate my guilt and fulfill the Christian law by attending church and giving money in place of self-sharing. In time, however, I will inevitably judge and condemn the members of the church as hypocrites, and I sell. **I am self-righteous;** I do not even have to leave the church to **sell my share.** I can remain a faithful attender and law-keeper having already alienated the other members in my affections.

Fused together in Christ's body (see Col. 1:18, 24), individual believers are called to "**be imitators of God** [*Father, Son, and Spirit: three Shareholders*], **as beloved children** [*re-gene-rating in Their fuse-able DNA*]; **and walk in Agape** [*incorruptible self-sharing Love*]" (Eph. 5:1-2). It is only in the *corpus* of the church—as Christ and not man defines *church*—that this practice and perfecting in Trinity-like Oneness can occur. We, as the *corpus* of Christ, are called to manifest the fusion glory of the Trinity by embodying Their kingdom cohabitation on the earth.

Bob Mumford said, "We have had 100 years of the church without the kingdom [*a corporation according to Worthless' design*]; **we dare not have the kingdom without the church** [*true incorporation in the corpus*]." If each and all would gather into the Nucleus of

Christ to magnify our Triune-God and **practice kingdom incorporation as self-sharers** rather than as individualists, what a mighty *Agape* reformation would take place in the church and in the earth! Let's carefully magnify the **relational blueprints** of this one shared estate together.

Father's Big-Family Dream

The eternal desire of the Father is a big family of unique sons and daughters who cohabit with Him in Oneness as self-sharers according to the eternal blueprints of the fusion of the Trinity. "For those whom He foreknew, He also predestined to become **conformed** [*morphed*] **to the image of His Son** [*perfected as a sacrificial Self-sharing Man*] so that He might be the firstborn among many [*re-gene-rated*] brethren" (Rom. 8:29). In a parable, Jesus represented the Father as saying, "Go out into the highways and along the hedges, and compel them to come in, so **that my house may be filled**" (Luke 14:23). Father wants to build (fuse, incorporate) us into His own house as "living stones" (1 Pet. 2:5). Jesus testified:

> [2]**In My Father's house are many dwelling places** [*room for each unique, fuse-able individual in one shared estate*]; if it were not so, I would have told you [*e.g. if it was a mirage based in "the lie" I would disclose it to you: Agape without hypocrisy*]; **for I**

go [*through the fission/fusion vortex of the cross*] **to prepare a place for you.** [3]**If I go and prepare a place for you** [*in My own body—the house Father and Spirit have chosen to dwell in*], I will come again and **receive you to Myself** [*into the Nucleus/ dwelling place of the Trinity*], **that where I AM** [*Father, Son, Spirit in Tri-unity*], **there you may be also** [*as sharers in the one shared life of God*]. [4]And you know **the way where I AM going** [*three Self-sharers in Christ embracing the cross in downward ascent*] (John 14:2-4).

Jesus' human body is Father's house! Within the crucified and resurrected body [*corpus*] of Christ, Father, Son, and Spirit are already waiting to receive us human beings as self-sharing members that we may **cohabit** together in one shared estate and fulfill Father's big-family dream. Very few have described this **reciprocal self-sharing** as accurately and masterfully as W. G. H. Holmes:

> No Christian can think of God save as He is unveiled and disclosed in Jesus Christ [*the Nucleus of the Trinity*].... Nor can he think of Jesus Christ, except as one to whom he has been mystically **united** [*fused*] by the Holy Spirit and thus **taken up into the Life of God** [*Most High*].... **It is in the Life of the Blessed Trinity that**

we live and move and have our being…a life of Love [*Agape: relational altruism*], which means an **eternal interchange of personal surrender of Self to Self** [*reciprocal Self-sharing*], so that Each penetrates and possesses the Others, three Consciousnesses that feel and think and will and perceive as one [*perichoresis*]. Into this Divine Life [*one shared estate*] the Christian has been **taken up**.

He that is in Christ [*abiding in fusion in the God-Man Nucleus*] is **surrendering himself** to the Father [*perpetual sacrificial self-sharing*] in the power of the Holy Spirit…which **gives him a share in the inner Life of God** [*sharing in the Life of three Self-sharers*]…our knowledge of the very Being of God, **the Trinity in Unity**, is disclosed and given to us in the Incarnation [*of the Son*] and by the outpouring of the Holy Spirit. Creatures are called to **share** in the inner movement [*fusion Vortex*] of Love within the Life of God.[1]

Through the Spirit, David perceived Father's big-family dream and *shared* in the Son's Own jealousy

---

[1] W. G. H. Holmes, *The Glory of God in the Incarnation of the Word*, p. 100-102

for Father's house: "**Zeal for Your house** [*Father's cohabitation of self-sharers*] **has consumed me** [*the individualist*]" (Ps. 69:9; John 2:17). This fiery zeal consumes all my own aspirations to be a proprietor in Worthless' world (*eros*), and all that remains is the Trinity's own desire to be a *self-sharer* burning within me—"**For the Lord your God** [*Father, Son, Spirit*] **is a consuming fire, a jealous God** [*jealous for One Another and for us*]" (Deut. 4:24). The Spirit of the Son expressed His Own **jealous zeal** for Father's big-family dream through the lyrics of David's *Song of Ascents* as he went up to the tent where Shekinah (the glory of the fusion of the Trinity) was resting upon the ark of covenant:

> [1]Behold, how **good** and how pleasant it is [*God's intended creation*] **for brothers** [*sharers of one bloodline: DNA-match*] **to dwell together in unity** [*fused as self-sharers into the Nucleus of our Elder Brother Jesus: the firstborn of a new creation*]! [2]It is like **the precious oil** [*the Spirit of Christ: fuse-able DNA*] upon the head [*Agape rationale— the mind of Christ*], **coming down** [*from the Triune-Most High*] upon the beard, even **Aaron's beard** [*e.g. Father-conscious priest-sons/daughters*], coming down upon the edge of his robes [*head-to-toe saturation: comprehensive re-gene-ration*]. [3]It is like **the dew of Hermon** [*a bountiful*

life-Source in the arid, fruitless wilderness of Worthless' world], coming down upon **the mountains of Zion** [*cohabitation of genuine self-sharers in Oneness*]; for **there** [*in Christ: the combined and combining God-Man*] **the Lord commanded the blessing** [*the shared, Family inheritance*]—**life forever** [*the one shared life of three, eternal Self-sharers opened to human beings*] (Ps. 133).

By faith, David saw forward to this cohabitation of self-sharers, and he was moved by God to establish a *physical* micro-model and temporary rehearsal studio of the *spiritual* kingdom called "Zion" (Ps. 2:6) in Jerusalem—"**a copy and shadow of the heavenly things**…according to **the pattern** [*blueprints*] which was shown you" (Heb. 8:5). In another Psalm of Ascents (downward ascent into God), David rejoiced that some of his people were also awakening *spiritually* and *relationally* to the reality of the kingdom of God and desired to emigrate into it with him:

¹I was glad when they said to me, "Let us go [*together*] to **the house of the Lord** [*cohabitation of three Self-sharers*]. ²Our feet are standing within your gates, O Jerusalem [*rehearsal studio of the eternal kingdom*], ³Jerusalem, that is **built as a city** [*cohabitation*] **that is compact together** [*e.g. one shared estate–self-sharers in fusion*]

Oneness; built according to the blueprints of the Trinity in Christ]; ⁴to which the tribes go up, even the tribes of the Lord—an **ordinance** for Israel [*relational, inter-personal Agape: the law of the kingdom*]— to **give thanks** to the name of the Lord [*reciprocate God's gene-rosity*]. ⁵For there, **thrones were set for judgment** [*to preserve justice: freedom and equality*], the thrones of the house of David [*upon which Jesus now sits, see Luke 1:32*].

⁶Pray for the **peace** of Jerusalem [*type of the kingdom in Christ: "Pray in this way '…Your kingdom come on earth as it is in heaven…'" Matt. 6:9*], **may they prosper who love you** [*kingdom economics: self-sharers gene-rously laying down their autonomous lives for one another yields superabundant bounty*].... ⁸**For the sake of my brothers and my friends** [*not for my own sake*], I will now say, "May peace be within you." ⁹**For the sake of the house of the Lord our God** [*zealously offering ourselves to God as a safe, eros-free cohabitation*], **I will** [*spend and expend myself to*] **seek your good** (Psalm 122).

Around 2000 B.C., **Abraham** saw "the city which has foundations, whose architect and builder is God"

(Heb. 11:10). Fourteen generations later (1000 B.C.; see Matt. 1:17), **David** saw the blueprints of this city and built the micro-model of *Zion* in Jerusalem. Twenty-eight generations later (95 A.D.), **John** also saw this eternal cohabitation which the Triune-God had prepared in Christ for mankind:

> And I saw **the holy city** [*cohabitation of self-sharers*], **new Jerusalem** [*fulfillment of the micro-model David built*], **coming down out of heaven from God** [*Most High: Three Who exalt One Another*], **made ready as a** [*many-membered*] **bride adorned** [*re-gene-rated in fuse-able DNA: born from above*] **for her husband** [*Triune-Groom: God in Christ*] (Rev. 21:2).

David saw the eternal blueprints of the kingdom of God—a relational infrastructure built of individual self-sharers—and he described this *cohabitation* as **a city that is compact together**. John described this city as one many-membered **bride**. What does this one shared estate look like and how does it come together?

Gardens Unlocked and Adjoining

"The Lord God planted a **garden** toward the east, in Eden; and there He [*the Triune-God, the Us*] placed the man whom He had formed" (Gen. 2:8). In the Garden of Eden, the Trinity purposed for the seed of Their own Self-sharing nature (*Agape*: relational altruism) to grow and mature in human beings, but it was aborted when man bought into the lie of individualism: self-worth-ship, self-will, and self-indulgence—relational fission. In **another garden, "Gethsemane"** (Matt. 26:36), the Son of God was perfected in the divine nature as a Man—a Prototype sacrificial Self-sharer—when He said, "Father…not My will, but Yours be done" (Luke 22:42). In the God-Man Jesus, Father, Son, and Spirit finally received **the first fruits of the harvest from the garden**—Their own *gene-rous* nature.

In the Song of Solomon, the tumultuous relationship between the bridegroom and his bride is a prophetic dress rehearsal illustrating Christ and us, His many-membered bride: "**A garden locked is my sister, my** [*many-membered*] **bride, a rock garden locked** [*in self-worth-ship, self-preservation*], **a spring sealed up** [*suppressing the flow of the Spirit within*]" (Song 4:12). We believers have been adopted by God through our Elder Brother Jesus Who is "the **firstborn** from the dead [*in self-love*]" (Col. 1:18), and "the **first fruits** of those who are asleep [*spiritually inebriated in* *self-worth-ship*]" (1 Cor. 15:20), and we are presently *re-gene-rating* in His bloodline; therefore, *collectively* we are Christ's "**sister**." However, we are not yet fully naturalized or mature in His *Agape* nature, we are not yet able to reciprocate His sacrificial self-sharing Love either God-ward or man-ward; therefore, *collectively*, we individual believers are not yet "**made ready as a** [*fused and fuse-able many-membered*] **bride**" (Rev. 21:2).

God has given each one of us the gift of individuality and free will: my own mind, my own heart, my own life (nucleus): **my own garden.** As an immature believer, I am still largely tyrannized by self-worth-ship; therefore, I spend all my time cultivating my garden *for* me. I only invite into my garden those whom I calculate will add to me, and I intentionally shut out those I estimate to be a liability. Hardened in self-interest, **I am a rock garden locked**. The kingdom remains eclipsed to those who seek to preserve their own garden in individualism: "For whoever wishes to **save his life** [*his own garden*] **will lose it** [*fission decay*]; but **whoever loses his life** [*as a sacrificial self-sharer*] **for My sake** [*the God-Man Nucleus*] **will find it** [*fused into the cohabitation of the Trinity and man: one shared estate*]" (Matt. 16:25).

Jesus said, "Behold, I **stand at the door** and knock; if anyone hears My voice and **opens the door**, I will come in to him and will dine with him, and he with Me [*reciprocal self-sharing*]" (Rev. 3:20). In Christ, God comes and stands outside **the locked gate** of each of our autonomous gardens. He calls to us in isolation and fission and famine within; He seeks to enter so that He may bring in with Him the bountiful kingdom. Initially, we are so eclipsed in individualism and imprisoned in self-worth-ship that we will only crack our gate wide enough to receive a seed through:

> [18][Jesus] was saying, "What is the **kingdom of God** [*three Self-sharers*] like, and to what shall I compare it? [19]It is like a mustard **seed** [*fuse-able DNA*], which a man [*individual*] took and threw into **his own garden** [*autonomous life*]; and it grew and became a tree, and the birds of the air nested in its branches [*inclusive hospitality*]" (Luke 13:18-19).

The kingdom of God is **one shared estate**: Father, Son, and Spirit, as free, Self-sharing Individuals, live eternally in One Another's **open, adjoining gardens;** therefore, "God is a dwelling place [*Three who mutually indwell One Another*]" (Deut. 33:27). According to the **relational blueprints** of the Trinity, the unlocked, open garden of each individual human being **adjoins** the unlocked gardens of other kingdom sons and daughters and becomes one shared estate: "behold, the kingdom of God is in your midst" (Luke 17:21). Our Triune-God does not merely want to live in us as individuals but in the one shared estate of **our adjoining** (fused) **lives**!

Consider these two mysteries: *first,* the entire kingdom estate, which the eternal Father, Son, and Spirit *are* and *share,* is contained within the **seed** of Christ! As an individualist and dispirited dirt-bag, when I intentionally receive this seed into the soil of my own garden, it begins to unlock and open: "for in this way [*reciprocal self-sharing*] the **entrance into the eternal kingdom** of our Lord and Savior Jesus Christ [*the God-Man Nucleus*] will be abundantly supplied to you [*one vast estate*]" (2 Pet. 1:11). *Second,* the entire kingdom estate, comprised of *our* individual, unlocked, adjoining gardens, is contained within the one, infinite God-Man Jesus:

> [2]Having been **knit** [*fused*] **together in Agape** [*the fuse-able DNA of three Self-sharers causes our individual gardens to unlock and adjoin*] and attaining to all the **wealth** [*superabundant bounty gene-rated from reciprocal self-sharing in one shared estate*] that comes from the full assurance of understanding [*the blueprints of the cohabitation of Father, Son, and Spirit as Self-sharers*]; resulting in a true knowledge of **God's mystery**, that is, **Christ Himself** [*the Trinity and mankind cohabit together in the corpus/Nucleus of the God-Man*] (Col. 2:2).

Though Christ has mercifully unlocked and opened my garden, and I am learning how to receive the Trinity and my brothers and sisters into it, **my garden remains my own** (see Acts 5:4). In this adjoining (fusion) of gardens, I do not lose the gift of my individuality; rather, as the seed of the three Self-sharers within me is nourished and cultivated, I am moved to **keep my garden open** in perpetual fusion. In fact, my garden never ceases to **expand** as I sacrificially accommodate more and more diverse people, even enemies, that I may serve and enrich them as a self-sharer—"the *Agape* of Christ controls us" (2 Cor. 5:14).

Clearly, one of the fundamental expressions of sacrificial self-sharing is "**practicing hospitality**" (Rom. 12:13). The Spirit orchestrates spontaneous life-labs to test, prove, reprove, and mature us as self-sharers: "Do not neglect to **show hospitality to strangers** [*a conduit of God's Self-sharing to all mankind*], for by this some have entertained angels without knowing it" (Heb. 13:2). To enter and participate in the one shared estate of the kingdom, there is no substitute for sharing my garden with those whom the Lord has entrusted into my care, but prepare yourself, **they will not all be angels!** To share in the kingdom of God, there is no short-cut around embracing the daily cross involved in keeping my garden open to all whom the Spirit brings through my garden gate.

Sharing my garden with others inevitably unearths and disturbs many hidden layers of proprietorship, entitlement, and control within me, and I grumble and complain in discontent because **my garden is not yet fully open**. It is easy to blame my own difficulty with sharing on those whom God brings into my garden, to find fault with them and disqualify them from entering my garden, but in truth, the problem is me. Paul urged, "O Corinthians, our heart is opened wide. You are not restrained by us, but you are **restrained in your own affections** [*self-worth-ship eclipses self-sharing*]. **Now in like exchange** [*reciprocal self-sharing*]—I speak as to children—**open wide to us also**" (2 Cor. 6:11-13). Peter urged us:

> 3:8All of you be **harmonious** [*Trinity-like*].... 4:8**Keep fervent in your** *Agape* **for one another** [*magnetized into fusion Oneness by sacrificial self-sharing Love*], **because** *Agape* **covers a multitude of sins** [*reverses the de-gene-rative effects of individualism, fission and con-fusion*]. 4:9**Be hospitable to one another** [*open your garden: your affections, time, home, food, and resources*] **without complaint** [*willingly and sacrificially paying the financial, material, and relational costs of receiving others into the Nucleus of Christ within you*]. 4:10**As each one** [*individual*] **has received a special gift** [*a unique aspect of the one, infinite Person of Christ*], **employ it** [*sacrificially invest it*] **in serving one another as good stewards of the**

manifold grace of God [*daily sharing together in the one shared estate the three Self-sharers have shared with us*] (1 Pet. 3:8, 4:8-10).

Sharing One Yoke

Father, Son, and Spirit *share* Their eternal kingdom with human beings and cohabit with us by **incorporating** each of our individual, unlocked gardens into **one shared estate** located within the **corpus** (body) of the combined and combining God-Man. As fellow heirs and **stewards** of this shared inheritance, we must learn to **cultivate** this one shared estate together as "**fellow workers for the kingdom of God**" (Col. 4:11). Paul described for us how self-sharers work together:

> [6]I planted, Apollos watered, but God was causing the growth. [7]So then neither the one who plants, nor the one who waters is anything [*e.g. we are not special; God choice of us is special*], but God who causes the growth [*by photosynthesis: yield of Triune-Light*]. [8]Now he who plants and he who waters are **one** [*yoked together in Christ*]; but each [*individual*] will receive his own reward according to his own labor. [9]For **we are God's fellow workers; you are God's field** [*lit. cultivated land; e.g. individual gardens incorporated into one*]

estate, one inheritance], **God's building** [*of living stones*] (1 Cor. 3:6-9).

First, Jesus taught us that **sharing one cross** with one another is essential to sharing one life. Second, as a practical analogy of that shared cross, Jesus teaches us that **sharing one yoke** is essential to becoming "fellow workers in Christ Jesus" (Rom. 16:3) who cultivate our one shared estate together and bring forth *generous* fruit:

> ²⁸Come to Me [*buy a share in the one estate of My body*], all who are **weary** and **heavy-laden** [*lit. work to exhaustion; e.g. enslaved in individualism*] and I will give you **rest** [*in the cohabitation of three Self-sharers*]. ²⁹**Take My yoke upon you** [*willingly embrace one shared life with God and one another*] and **learn from Me** [*Trinity-like Agape: how to live and work together as imitators of God*], for I am gentle and humble in heart [*Self-emptied: a Nucleus perfected in downward ascent*], and you will **find rest for your souls** [tyrannized by self-will]. ³⁰For **My yoke** [*sacrificial self-sharing*] **is easy** and **My burden** [*reciprocal burden-bearing*] **is light** (Matt. 11:28-30).

The *cross* and the *yoke* that Christ shares with us are synonymous—both are made of wood from the tree of life. **One yoke is built for two necks**; it is designed to enable two burden-bearers to walk, work, and live together equitably, efficiently, and with far greater productivity and joy than would be possible alone. Each individual believer shares one yoke with Christ, and in Himself (the corpus), Christ yokes each of us individual believers together with one another. The yoke Jesus bore as a Man was doing all things as a Self-sharer with the Father in the Spirit:

> **[17]My Father is working** until now, and **I Myself am working** [*co-laborers and Stewards of one shared estate*] [19]… **the Son can do nothing of Himself** [*autonomously*], unless it is something He sees the Father doing; for whatever the Father does, these things the Son also does **in like manner** [*in one shared yoke*] (John 5:17, 19).

Willingly bearing one yoke together as free individuals is **the secret of true authority**: "Then God [*three incorruptible Stewards, burden-Bearers*] said, 'Let Us make **man** in Our [*Self-sharing*] image, according to Our [*fuse-able*] likeness; and **let them rule** [*as self-emptied stewards who share the burden, work, and authority of one shared estate*]…'" (Gen. 1:26). According to Their own design, these three Self-sharers who created and redeemed us have purposed to **yoke us in the one Spirit of Christ Jesus**: "…be subject to one another in the fear of Christ" (Eph. 5:21).

At first this yoke seriously chafes the flesh and a **powerful instinct of self-preservation** surges up from within to pull my neck out and run back inside my locked garden. It is Worthless' *de-gene-rate* nature and instinct of **individualism** in me that would rather starve to death in *famine* than to embrace the shared yoke and inherit the *bounty* of one shared estate. Before Stephen was stoned, he testified, "You men who are **stiff-necked** and uncircumcised in heart and ears are always **resisting the Holy Spirit**; you are doing just as your fathers did" (Acts 7:54).

It is all too easy for Worthless, the father of the lie, to convince us inebriated individualists that this yoke, which Jesus died to be able to *share* with us, is a yoke of slavery that will control, chafe, and **severely limit us** from going, doing, acquiring, and owning what we want. This is a shrewd deception indeed, since it is true "the *Agape* [*one shared yoke*] of Christ **controls us**" (2 Cor. 5:14). Embracing and bearing this yoke certainly means "**that you may not do the things that you please** [*indulging me now at the expense of others*]" (Gal. 5:17). However, the truth that the false-father Worthless shrewdly *withholds* from us is this: to *reject* Jesus' yoke of self-sharing means **I must bear Worthless' yoke of slavery by default**. Yoked to this self-deceived deceiver, I chase one mirage after another on a path of upward descent into fission, futility, and famine:

It was for **freedom** that **Christ set us free** [*to freely participate as self-sharers in the kingdom*]; therefore keep standing firm [*abiding in Jesus' yoke*] and do not be subject again to a **yoke of slavery** [*self-worth-ship, self-will, self-indulgence*] (Gal. 5:1).

Ultimately, there is only one thing powerful enough to *move* me, as a recovering individualist, to willingly keep my stiff neck in one shared yoke with you, the annoying, trying brother whom God has called me to love and that *motivator* is "**faith working through *Agape***" (Gal. 5:6). Faith enables me to *see* Father, Son, and Spirit as **three burden-Bearers yoked together in Christ**. Faith enables me to *recognize* that even now They are among us laboring to *re-gene-rate* us as sharers in Their own shared estate!

By faith, I *know* that the Triune-God entered Worthless' world in Christ Jesus, "the Son of Man," and intentionally **yoked Themselves to you and to me** and to all *de-gene-rate* mankind in Agape for better or worse, in life and in death. The gift of this *faith* and *knowledge* I have received is **altruism**—the only *true* and *gen-uine* thing to be found anywhere in Worthless' world, and it is only found here because Triune-*Agape* came down to us from above, first in the incarnated Son and now in the Holy Spirit.

¹²**If we Agape one another** [*practice reciprocal, sacrificial self-sharing: embracing one yoke*], **God** [*Father, Son, Spirit: one Dwelling Place*] **abides in us**, and His *Agape* [*fuse-able DNA*] is perfected in us. ¹³By this we know that **we abide in Him and He in us** [*one shared life in one estate*], because He has given us of **His Spirit** [*Spirit-sharing Love*]. ¹⁴We have seen and testify that the **Father has sent the Son** to be the Savior of the world [*Son-sharing Love*] (1 John 4:12-14).

As I *appraise* the **one shared life** of God in Christ and *worth-ship* how these three burden-Bearers are yoked together in this Self-sharing Man, I am moved to *forsake* self-worth-ship and *buy into* Their **one shared estate** by embracing Their **one shared yoke** with you, my brother. It is not possible to share one yoke with Christ without also being **yoked to you, my brother**, who is His own treasured inheritance entrusted to me and shared with me. If I choose to *embrace* this yoke with you, and if I learn from Jesus how to live and labor together with you in gentleness and humility day by day, and if I don't quit or cast it off, not only does this yoke become easy as He promised but **I come to cherish our yoke** as the essential means of sharing one life together with you, my brother, in the one shared estate of God in Christ.

The inexpressible joy of being yoked together with you in Christ as reciprocal self-sharers and bearing fruit together as God's fellow workers, causes me to reflect on my former selfish, fruitless life in a garden locked and seriously "hate my own life in this world" (John 12:25). In fact, I never want to look back! Jesus said, "**No one, after putting his hand to the plow** [*e.g. embracing one yoke*] **and looking back** [*to his own autonomous, locked garden*], **is fit for the kingdom of God** [*one shared estate*]" (Luke 9:62). T. Austin Sparks taught us how to overcome the difficulties we experience in being yoked together:

> It is so easy to allow **unworthy considerations** [*self-consciousness, self-worth-ship*], to quench brotherly love [*the risk and spontaneity of Agape*], to be clogged up with resentment or be wrongly influenced by our susceptibilities or hurt feelings…. We have to be **active in positive cultivation of fellowship** [*relational fusion*]. To some it is quite natural to be independent [*an individualist*]. For them **deference to others** represents a major difficulty…they just **prefer to do it alone** and never seriously think of **inter-relatedness** and **inter-dependence** [*reciprocal self-sharing*]. The Word of God, however, is most explicit in ordering us to **esteem one another**, to submit to one

another and to **live and work together** [*embracing one shared yoke in Trinity-likeness*]. The Holy Spirit demands that the people of God live according to a **team order of things**, that they should be **governed by a family spirit** [*the law of Agape*].

Anything which is of an **isolated or detached nature** [*fission*], which fails to recognize and fully accept **the family thought of God** [*Father's big family dream*], is a check on Him. By failing to observe fellowship [*reciprocal self-sharing*] we quench the Spirit [*the Re-gene-rator*]. It is not only a matter of avoiding giving offense but of **active pursuit of fellowship** [*fusion Oneness*]. Some may be wondering why there is so little up-springing of life from the inner well [*drought and famine*], when they are sitting back in a wrong kind of modesty, **failing to bring in their own personal contribution** [*sacrificial self-sharing*] to fellowship life and ministry [*co-laborers in one shared estate*]… Get in, get right in, and let yourself go![2]

---

[2] T. Austin Sparks, *The Well Within* From "Toward the Mark" July-August 1976, Vol. 5-4. Retrieved from http://www.austin-sparks.net/english/000472.html.

All Things in Common

The first church described in the book of Acts is the most awe-inspiring, practical, real-life example of how individual believers become sharers with one another in the **one shared estate** of our Triune-God. The account of this prototype congregation provides detailed blueprints that reveal how we are to *grow* together as self-sharing members of the body (*corpus*) of Christ and therefore *serve* together as the **embodiment** of the kingdom of God on earth. This first *corpus* began with "one hundred and twenty persons" (Acts 1:15), including the eleven remaining disciples who scattered in fission from Jesus at His arrest but whom He gathered into Himself again in the days between His resurrection and ascension.

> ¹When the day of Pentecost had come, they were **all together in one place.** ²And suddenly there came from heaven a noise like a **violent rushing wind** [*Vortex of the Triune-Pneuma*], and it filled the whole house [*cohabitation*] where they were sitting. ³And there appeared to them **tongues** [*vortices*] **of fire** distributing themselves, and they rested on each one of them. ⁴And they were **all filled with the Holy Spirit** [*the Re-gene-rator: one, fuse-able DNA*] and began speaking with other tongues, as the Spirit was giving them utterance (Acts 2:1-4).

These one hundred and twenty persons who shared this encounter were remarkably **diverse individuals**. Among them was a former **tax collector**, Matthew, who exacted wealth from his own people for the Roman Empire, and sitting next to him in this one place was "Simon the Zealot" (Acts 1:13), a **revolutionary** who sought to overthrow Rome's tyranny over Israel! There were also **religious Jews** who believed in Jesus, perhaps even scribes and Pharisees sitting beside a former **prostitute**, Mary Magdalene, "from whom Jesus had cast out seven demons" (Mark 16:9). Among these individualists who had, in various ways, become "conformed [*lit. summorphos, morphed*] to this world" (Rom. 12:2), the **common denominator** was that each and all believed "truth is in Jesus" (Eph. 4:21).

These radically diverse persons were **baptized** individually and collectively into Father, Son, and Spirit—**fused** together by the Vortex of the Triune-Pneuma into one God-Man Nucleus. Therefore, as members of the *corpus* of the resurrected, ascended Christ, and as sharers in the one Spirit whom Father and Son shared with them and appointed to remain with them, each and all were **relocated** together into the eternal kingdom even while sitting together in that room on the earth! Later, Paul was also incorporated into this *corpus* and testified:

> [4]But God [*Father, Son, Spirit*] [5]...made us alive together with Christ [*members of His*

resurrected corpus] [6]…and raised us up with Him [*the Triune-Most High*], and **seated us with Him in the heavenly places in Christ Jesus** [*the God-Man Nucleus*]. [18]… for through Him [*the Son*], we both [*Jew and Gentile*] have our access **in one Spirit** to the Father [*the third heaven*] (Eph. 2:4-6, 18).

As fellow-emigrants, these one hundred and twenty persons embarked upon a *spiritual* journey into the most wondrous heavenly life of Trinity-like Oneness, a life of **reciprocal self-sharing** that they lived out in very *practical* ways in their daily life.

[44]And all those who had believed were **together** [*fused into the God-Man Nucleus; incorporated into the corpus*] and **had all things in common** [*sharers in one shared estate*]; [45]and they began selling their property and possessions [*dismantling their autonomous lives*] and were **sharing** them with all, as anyone might have need [*us-consciousness displacing me-consciousness*]. [46]Day by day continuing with **one mind** in the temple, and **breaking bread** [*the fusion fuel of God in Christ*] **from house to house** [*unlocked, adjoining gardens*], they were taking their meals together with gladness and sincerity of heart [*Agape without hypocrisy*], [47]praising God and

having favor with all the people. And the Lord was adding to their number day by day those who were being saved (Acts 2:44-47).

Father, Son, and Spirit granted these believers a share in Their one shared estate; this is called **perichoresis**: mutual indwelling and interpenetration without loss of personal identity. The dynamic activity of the kingdom of the Triune-God was being expressed on the earth through the church, the many-membered *corpus* of Christ—individual self-sharers moving from one unlocked, adjoining garden to another, eating Jesus together, and manifesting the glory of the Triune-Life.

> [32]And the congregation of those who believed were of **one heart** and **soul** [*fused into the corpus of Christ*]; and not one of them claimed that anything belonging to him was his own [*forfeiting individualism, self-worth-ship, proprietorship*], but **all things were common property** to them [*one shared estate*]. [33]And with great power [*fusion*] the apostles were giving testimony to the resurrection of the Lord Jesus, and **abundant grace was upon them all** [*reciprocal self-sharing gene-rates superabundant bounty*]. [34]For there was **not a needy person among them**, for all who were owners of land or houses

would **sell** them and bring the proceeds of the sales [35]and lay them at the apostles' feet [*mammon entrusted to self-emptied, incorruptible stewards*], and they would be **distributed** to each as any had need [*Triune-Justice: preserving freedom and equality*] (Acts 4:32-35).

Do not overlook the fact that in the living *corpus* of the God-Man Jesus Christ these believers were not only sharing life with one another, but they were also in daily **fellowship with Father, Son, and Spirit.** John testified,

> [2]The eternal life, which was with the Father and was manifested to us [*first in Christ, then in the Spirit*] [3]…that you too may have fellowship with **us;** and indeed our fellowship is with the Father, and with His Son Jesus Christ (1 John 1:2-3).

Daily exposure to Triune-Light that caused these individuals to grow together as self-sharers and become **acculturated into the one shared life of the Trinity.**

Recognizing the full context of their life with God in Christ, we begin to understand what motivated these first believers to systematically dismantle their autonomous, independent lives in this world and build one relational life in Jesus. Once an individual truly sacrificially shares **self** with others in the estate of the Triune-God, sharing his own **material things** is no longer the costly sacrifice he previously calculated it to be:

> ¹The churches…⁴begging us with much urging for the favor of **participation** [*sharing*] in the support of the saints [*in famine*] ⁵…but they **first gave themselves to the Lord and to us by the will of God** [*three Self-sharers*] (2 Cor. 8:1-5).

The fusion of individual believers as sacrificial self-sharers into Christ's body (*corpus*) is **the church**. Abiding together with Father, Son, and Spirit in sustained fusion (reciprocal self-sharing) in this one *corpus*—moving as one in the Vortex of the Triune-Spirit—releases the authority, power, and bounty of **the kingdom** on earth. The first church in Jerusalem and the first Gentile church in Antioch (see Acts 11:26) **embodied** the kingdom and became conduits of this power. The Spirit cultivated and established these believers as local **fusion reactors** that *produced* far more energy, Light, and Life than they consumed. Reciprocal self-sharing (*Agape*) is *gene-rative*, fusion power that yields exponential multiplication and bounty.

Unbelievers who are living as *de-gene-rate* individualists in the **eclipse** of Worthless' world but who gain exposure to the kingdom of three Self-sharers embodied in the church feel the heat and **the Light** among *gen-uine* **believers** whom they see *gene-rously* sharing all things. These lost sons and daughters are magnetized to fuse themselves into God in Christ through the *corpus* of the church. We must ask, why would anyone want to "lose his life" (Matt. 16:25) to buy a share in a church that does not embody the kingdom? In other words, who would be moved to unlock, open, and sacrificially share his own garden amidst a group of rock gardens that may border one another but are locked and divided by electric fences for security? A local congregation of believers is merely a "**lampstand**, so that those who enter [*the church*] may see the light [*of the kingdom*]" (Luke 11:33). Jesus rebuked His church (*corpus*) at Ephesus:

> Therefore remember from where you have fallen [*out of the kingdom cohabitation of God Most High: Three Who exalt and add to One Another*] and repent and do the deeds you did at first [*reciprocal self-sharing*]; or else I am coming to you and will remove your **lampstand** out of its place [*since it is no longer the true corpus: God and man in fusion in Christ*] (Rev. 2:5).

Immediately following the Vortex of the Triune-Pneuma—the outpouring of the Holy Spirit upon the first church—**exponential fusion** took place: "Those who received his [*Peter's*] word [*testimony of God in Christ*] were baptized [*fused into Father, Son, and Spirit*]; and that day there were **added** [*incorporated into the corpus of Christ*] about three thousand souls" (Acts 2:41). Subsequently, through the book of

Acts, Father's house was continually being filled as "considerable numbers [*lit. crowds*] were brought [*added*] **to the Lord** [*given a share in the one shared estate of three Self-sharers*]" (Acts 11:24).

The movie entitled "A Good Year" (Twentieth Century Fox, 2006) profoundly illustrates the dynamics of individualism, corporations, locked gardens, and one shared estate. The main character "Max," played by Russell Crowe, is a shrewd London stockbroker enslaved in the corporate world by greed and **opportunism**. Max inherits the estate and winery of his deceased uncle in France where he spent summers as a boy. As a self-absorbed individualist, Max devalued and marginalized his uncle in the ten years before his death, a man who truly loved him and wanted him to inherit the estate along with the one shared life it represented but knew his nephew had become deeply selfish.

Max returns to France and with calloused indifference seeks to quickly **sell the estate**. However, Max falls in love with "Fanny" and invites her to relocate to London with him. Fanny answers, "How typical to assume that I live in Provence because I have no other choice." He replies, "Fanny, this place just doesn't suit my life." She responds, "No, Max. **It is your life** [*of individualism, opportunism*] **that doesn't suit this place** [*one shared estate*]." Like the prodigal son, Max must awaken from self-worth-ship to discern his true inheritance and cherish it as a self-sharer.

In the next volume, *God Magnified Part 10: Observing Justice and Equality*, we will examine Pillar 12: "**the Lord is a God of justice**" (Isa. 30:18) and discover how true justice issues forth from these three sacrificial Self-sharers Who preserve the **freedom** and **equality** of all whom They receive into the cohabitation of Their own kingdom. We will see how Triune-Justice and the eternal "law" of *Agape* is revealed and demonstrated in the Man Jesus—**the Equalizer** who raised a standard of individual **integrity** (godliness) that facilitates *relational* **integration** (Trinity-like fusion) and prevents **disintegration** (fission).

Jesus observed, "The kingdom of heaven [*one shared estate*] **suffers violence** [*lit. is forcibly entered*] **and violent men** [*opportunists*] **take it by force** [*lit. seize it for themselves*]" (Matt. 11:12). Our Triune-God has redeemed us individualists out of Worthless' world, adopted us, and brought us Home into Themselves. In this one shared estate, **justice** ensures that we half-formed children of God **respect one another's unlocked gardens** (individuality)—that we do not forcibly enter the garden of another with **entitlement** to take, abuse, or control; rather, we enter as self-sharers bearing gifts to add, to honor, and to build. Paul recognized that justice, freedom, equality, peace, and fruit-bearing are only possible among individual believers as we are **fused together in the corpus of Christ**:

[13]Until we [*together*] attain to **the unity of the faith** [*perfected in fusion Oneness in Christ just as Father, Son, and Spirit are One in Christ*], and of the knowledge of the Son of God [*the God-Man Nucleus*], to **a mature man** [*one functional many-membered body–sharing one nature, name, purpose*], to the measure of the stature which belongs to the **fullness of Christ.** [15]...we are to **grow up in all aspects into Him** [*an us in the image and likeness of the Us*] who is the head, even Christ, [16]from whom the whole body, being fitted and **held together by what every joint supplies** [*reciprocal Agape*], according to **the proper working** [*sacrificial self-sharing*] **of each individual part**, causes the growth of **the body** for the building up of itself [*the corpus of the kingdom*] in *Agape* [*the strong Nuclear force*] (Eph. 4:13-16).

One Nucleus, One Man, One Body

A film entitled "Enemy At the Gates" (Paramount Pictures, 2001) is based on the true story of an uneducated Russian named Vassili Zaitsev (played by Jude Law) who became a skilled Soviet sniper in the brutal confrontation of Nazi and Soviet forces at

Stalingrad in World War 2. Joseph Fiennes plays an educated, Soviet political officer who publishes the accounts of Vassili's kills as propaganda to keep up the morale among soldiers who were literally being forced to forfeit their lives to withstand further Nazi invasion. Due to Vassili's success in killing German commanders and delaying their victory, a famous Nazi sniper (played by Ed Harris) is sent to bait Vassili and kill him.

In the midst of this struggle, the educated Soviet political officer becomes jealous of Vassili and begins to use his influence to destroy him. However, the officer recognizes his own **toxic envy,** and in repentance, goes to the place Vassili is waiting in concealment for the superior Nazi sniper and says to him:

> I've been such a fool, Vassili. Man will always be man [*e.g. de-gene-rate, corrupt*]. There is no **new man** [*Soviet dictum/motto: one new man*]. We tried so hard to **create a society that was equal**, where there'd be nothing to **envy your neighbor**. But there's always something to envy. A smile, a friendship. Something you don't have and **want to appropriate** [*e.g. corruption: I want; I will have; I deserve to have*]. In this world—even a Soviet one—there will always be rich and poor. Rich in gifts, poor in gifts. Rich in love, poor in love. I want to help you Vassili. One last thing;

something useful for a change, let me show you where the German Major is.

In the hiding place, the Russian political officer leans forward, exposing himself into open view, and immediately the German sniper mistakes him for Vassili and shoots him through the head. This act reveals the German sniper's position and provides Vassili opportunity to locate and kill him. The one new man of the Soviet Union was proven to be a **counterfeit** because it was comprised of *de-gene-rate*, self-promoting individualists pulling one another down in the crab-bucket of Worthless' world. Curiously, it is the **sacrificial self-giving act** of laying down his life for Vassili that is the secret to the **genuine one new man:**

> [13]**In Christ Jesus** [*the God-Man Nucleus*] you who formerly were afar off [*individualists in fission*] have been brought near by the blood of Christ [*a new bloodline: fuse-able DNA*]. [14]For He Himself is our peace [*Nucleus of relational fusion*], who made both groups [*Jews and Gentiles*] into one and broke down the barrier of the dividing wall, [15]by abolishing in His flesh the enmity [*corruption, relational fission, injustice*]... so that **in Himself** He might make the two into **one new man**, thus establishing peace [*freedom, equality, justice*], [16]and

might reconcile them both **in one body** to God through the cross by having put to death the enmity. [18]...for through Him [*the God-Man*] we both have our access in one Spirit to the Father [*e.g. "the third heaven" 2 Cor. 12:2*].

[19]So then you are no longer strangers and aliens, but you are **fellow citizens** [*cohabiters*] with the saints [*lit. holy ones; sacrificial self-sharers*], and are **of God's household** [*incorporated into the Home/ Nucleus of "the Lord of hosts"*], [20]having been built on the foundation of the apostles and prophets [*forerunners into the kingdom*], **Christ Jesus Himself being the corner stone** [*God-Man Nucleus of Triune-Solidarity*], [21]in whom the whole building, being fitted [*fused*] together, is **growing into a holy temple in the Lord** [*within the eternal cohabitation of three Self-sharers*], [22]in whom you also are being built [*fused*] together into **a dwelling of God in the Spirit** (Eph. 2:13-22).

Among the major themes theologians identify and highlight in the Scriptures, I believe the primary, over-arching theme is **one Nucleus, one man, one body** (*many-membered corpus*). Jesus said to the religious Jews, "You search **the Scriptures** because you think that in them you have eternal life; it is these that **testify about Me** [*the God-Man Nucleus*]; and you are **unwilling to come to Me** [*e.g. lose your autonomous life into God in Christ*] that you may have life [*one shared life in one shared estate: the eternal kingdom*]" (John 5:39-40). John's Book of Revelation is literally "the revelation of Jesus Christ, [*e.g. blueprints*] which God gave him to show His bondservants..." (Rev. 1:1).

The **blueprints** of the infrastructure of the kingdom of God are revealed from various perspectives and illustrated in many unique ways through the 66 books of the Old and New Testaments. Working from macro to micro, we have looked at how individual **stars** encompass the nucleus of one galaxy and move together in the swirling arms of this vortex; and individual, unlocked **gardens** adjoin one another and become one shared estate; and **living stones** are fit together on one Cornerstone and become one building. Now, let's continue magnifying the blueprints of this cohabitation as they are rolled out before us through the following Scriptures, so we may see and understand how you and I, as individual **members**, are incorporated into the one body (corpus) of one Man. Zechariah prophesied:

> [12]Thus says **the Lord of hosts**, "Behold, a man whose name is **Branch**, for He will branch out from where He is [*Son of*

the Triune-God]; and He will **build the temple of the Lord** [*cohabitation of God and man in His own body*]. [13]...and He who will bear the honor and sit and rule on His throne. Thus, **He will be a priest on His throne** [*a sacrificial Self-sharing Minister to God and man*], and the counsel of **peace** will be between the two offices [*King and Priest*]" (Zech. 6:12-13).

At the dedication of the Temple in Jerusalem, Solomon prayed, "But **will God indeed dwell** [*cohabit*] **with mankind on the earth**? Behold, heaven and the highest heaven cannot contain You; how much less this house [*physical rehearsal studio*] which I have built" (2 Chron. 6:18). The eternal Father, Son, and Spirit mutually indwell One Another, cohabiting in the nest of rest of One Another's vulnerable, Self-sharing Love. However, for the Triune-God to dwell with mankind on the earth as the Lord of hosts, **a Human Nucleus** was required—a *corpus* into which mankind could be *incorporated*. T. Austin Sparks described this infinite, all-encompassing God-Man as "**the combined and combining Person** of our Lord Jesus Christ."[3]

When He [**the Son**] comes into the world [*as a Man*], He says, "Sacrifice and

---

[3] Sparks, T. Austin (n.d.) *The Testimony of the Christ*, Chapter 7 – "A Corporate Vessel of the Testimony." Retrieved from http://www.austin-sparks.net/english/books/002986.html.

offering You have not desired [*e.g. God is not a taker–an exacting Proprietor or Judge*], but **a body** [*a many-membered corpus/ cohabitation*] **You have prepared for Me** [*as the consummate sacrificial Self-sharer*]" (Heb. 10:5).

The ultimate purpose for which the Trinity sacrificed Themselves in Christ at the Cross was not merely to bear the penalty of our sin in our place for our justification, but also **to prepare a many-membered body in a God-Man**—a Home suitable for the cohabitation of the Triune-God and human beings. In Christ Jesus, the Trinity exhausted into Themselves the full power of our **relational fission** in order to make **relational fusion** possible for us, that we, as "a new [*fuse-able*] creation" (Gal. 6:15), could be **incorporated into the corpus** of this God-Man. Jesus said to Peter, "**If I do not wash you** [*of eros individualism, self-worth-ship*], **you have no part with Me** [*e.g. as a member in the cohabitation of My body*]" (John 13:8). Paul referred to the incorporation (fusion) of the Lord God of hosts and human beings in the body of one God-Man as "**the summing up of all things in Christ**" (Eph. 1:10). Paul also assured us that "We know that if the **earthly tent** [*physical body*] which is our house is torn down [*decays and dies: a corpse*], we have a building from God [*the God-Man corpus*], **a house not made with hands**, eternal in the heavens" (2 Cor. 5:1). Paul added, "Though our **outer** man [*tent, body, corpus*] is decaying [*in corruption*], our **inner man** [*spirit*] is being renewed day by day [*re-gene-rated in the incorruptible, fuse-able DNA of Christ*]" (2 Cor. 4:16).

John saw the cohabitation, which God sacrificially prepared for us in Christ, and declared, "This is **God's commandment** [*the Law of three Self-sharers*], **that we believe in the name of His Son Jesus Christ** [*buy into the God-Man Nucleus*], **and Agape one another** [*share one name and one life in His one body*]" (1 John 3:23). Paul added, "The Gentiles [*non-Jews*] are **fellow heirs** and **fellow members** [*sharers*] **of the body** [*corpus of Christ*] and **fellow partakers** [*sharers*] of the promise in Christ Jesus through the gospel [*invitation to share in the life of three Self-sharers as heirs of God and fellow heirs with Christ*]" (Eph. 3:6). The declarations of both John and Paul make evident that we who desire to participate in the cohabitation of the God-Man Jesus must learn to receive and reciprocate *Agape* (sacrificial self-sharing Love) not only God-ward but also with one another as fellow members of the one body. Dale Aukerman explained:

> **God** [*Father, Son, Spirit*], in order that we might meet Him, narrowed Himself down **into Jesus** [*the human Nucleus of the Trinity*]. But Jesus was also the narrowing down of the totality of **humankind** [*the Nucleus of human beings*]. He was formed [*incarnated as the Son of Man*] that our

vision might rest not only on this focal expression of the invisible God but also on **this singular image of the neighbors we have been too nearsighted** [*self-focused*] **to see** and the myriads of human beings [*in other nations and past and future ages*] we have no sight to see...we are to see Him [*Christ Jesus, the Lord of hosts*] who is focus and head of that vast throng.[4]

David prophesied that the coming God-Man would not merely embody the cohabitation of human beings with God, but He would also be the Nucleus of our fusion oneness with one another:

> [1]**He who dwells in the shelter** [*Nucleus/ body*] **of the Most High** [*"Jesus, Son of the Most High God" Luke 1:32*] **will abide in the shadow of the Almighty** [*cohabit with the All-Three-Mighty in Christ*]. [2]I will say to the Lord [*of hosts*], "My refuge and my fortress, my God [*Triune-Solidarity*], in whom I trust!".... [4]He will cover you with His pinions, and **under His wings** you may seek refuge [*in the nest of rest of the Triune-Spirit*]; His **faithfulness** [*all-true Love of Father, Son, Spirit*] is a shield and a bulwark.... [9]For you [*my brother*]

---

[4] Dale Aukerman, "The Central Murder," *Sojourners*, March 1980.

have made the Lord, **my refuge**, even the Most High, **your dwelling place** [*Nucleus of the relational oneness of you and me as fellow heirs with Christ*]. (Ps. 91:1-9).

Each individual believer who has bought into Christ at the cost of his own autonomy ("loses his life" Matt. 16:25) must learn to *share* the one Life of the Trinity ("all things" Rom. 8:32) with other believers in the Nucleus of Christ's one body as members of one new man. Paul made this **man-ward dimension** of reciprocal self-sharing in the kingdom abundantly clear:

> [12]For even as **the body is one** and yet has **many members**, and all the members of the body, though they are many [*unique individuals*], are one body, so also is **Christ** [*the combined and combining God-Man*]. [13]For by one Spirit [*the Re-gene-rator*] **we were all baptized in one body** [*buried and resurrected into one Man; incorporated into one corpus; fused into one Nucleus in Trinity-like fusion*]…and we were all made to drink of one Spirit [*Who plants and cultivates the fuse-able DNA of Christ within each of us*]. [14]For the body is not one member [*an individualist*], but many….

²²The members of the body which seem to be weaker are necessary; ²³and those members of the body which we deem less honorable, on these we bestow more **abundant honor** [*Agape rationale: downward ascent*].... ²⁵so that there may be **no division** [*relational fission*] **in the body, but that the members may have the same care for one another** [*reciprocal, sacrificial self-sharing: Trinity-likeness, the bedrock of true justice*]. ²⁶And if one member suffers, all the members suffer with it; if one member is honored, all the members rejoice with it. ²⁷Now **you are Christ's body, and individually members of it** (1 Cor. 12:12-27).

To function as an *incorporated* member within the *corpus* of Christ, clearly an individual must become a self-sharer. It is also evident that **sacrificial self-sharing requires self-denial**: to truly *share* myself, I must be capable of *denying* myself. "Jesus was saying to them all, 'If anyone wishes to come after Me, he must **deny himself**, and take up his cross daily [*put to death the old, de-gene-rate, self-indulgent man*] and follow Me [*in downward Ascent*]' " (Luke 9:23). You and I were not born with the capacity to deny and share ourselves; therefore, we must be "**born again** [*lit. born from above*]" (John 3:3). Each one of us must be **re-gene-rated** in the self-sharing image and fuse-able likeness of Father, Son, and Spirit as "partakers [*sharers*] of the divine nature [*Agape DNA*]" (2 Pet. 1:4).

In self-preservation, Peter denied the Triune-God in Christ three times saying, "**I do not know the man**!" (Matt. 26:74). You and I must **deny *self*** in this very same way. Paul set an example for us: "I have been crucified with Christ [*co-crucifixion*]; and **it is no longer I** [*the de-gene-rate individualist*] **who lives** [*e.g. I do not know that man—"the old self"*], **but Christ lives in me**" (Gal. 2:20). What exactly is it that could possibly motivate us to daily act *against* self and repeatedly make this exchange? The answer is receiving and reciprocating "**the zeal of the Lord**" (Isa. 9:7), which is a passionate manifestation and radical expression of *Agape*. When Jesus drove out all the religious mercenaries "who were buying and selling in the Temple [*God's house in the midst of Israel*]" (Matt. 21:12), His disciples remembered David's prophetic words, "**Zeal for Your house** [*Father's cohabitation of self-sharers*] **has consumed me** [*eliminated me: the individualist*]" (Ps. 69:9; John 2:17).

Zeal is the reciprocal magnetism of *Agape* that motivates each individual from within to perpetually abide as a sacrificial self-sharer in fusion Oneness with God and others. Zeal for Father's house consumes (purges, sanctifies, and eradicates) my *eros* individualism: my default mode of self-worth-ship and habits of opportunism. "For the Lord your **God is**

a consuming fire, a jealous God [*Father, Son, Spirit jealous/zealous for One Another and for us*]" (Deut. 4:24). As I encounter and consistently embrace this consuming fire—receive and reciprocate the *zeal* of Triune-*Agape*—all that remains of me is a free, fuse-able, Trinity-like individual. Though the Spirit of God works this in me, no one can do it for me; reciprocating the zeal of the Lord must be my own daily, volitional, intentional act. Paul wrote:

> [9]You laid aside the **old self** with its evil [*corrupt, self-indulgent*] practices, [10]and have put on the **new self** [*fuse-able DNA of Christ*] who is being renewed [*lit. renovated; re-gene-rated, matured*] to a true knowledge [*of Triune-Agape*] according to **the image of the One** [*the Us in Oneness, Gen. 1:26*] **who created him** [*a free individual created to voluntarily, perpetually, and zealously share himself in relational fusion*]– [11]a renewal [*re-gene-ration*] in which there is **no distinction** between Greek and Jew [*racial*], circumcised and uncircumcised [*religious*], barbarian, Scythian [*cultural sophistication*], slave and freeman [*social class*], but **Christ is all, and in all** [*one new, many-membered Man*].

> [14]Put on *Agape*, which is **the perfect bond of unity** [*lit. the uniting bond of perfection;*

fuse-able DNA]. [15]Let the peace of Christ rule in your hearts [*choose to abide in relational rest*], to which indeed you were called **in one body** [*incorporated into one corpus of self-sharers*]; and be **thankful** [*e.g. remembering the privilege of this shared inheritance prevents me from lapsing into individualism*] (Col. 3:9-15).

"Christ's body, which is the church" (Col. 1:18, 24) is comprised of individual believers called together to replicate the reciprocal Self-sharing dynamic of Father, Son, and Spirit and therefore manifest the fusion glory of the Triune-God by **embodying** the cohabitation of Their kingdom on the earth. T. Austin Sparks described the practical implications of becoming a member of this one, many-membered man:

> **Christ is not a second personality or power**, to come along to reinforce *us* [*e.g. me*], to vivify *us*, to strengthen *us*, for us to use in life and service, and that He should make *us* something. That is not the thought, and that is not the angle of Scripture at all. And yet, how almost universally, perhaps largely unconsciously, that is what is happening. **Christians are wanting to be made something**, even as Christians; and Christian workers and the Lord's servants are, though

perhaps unwittingly, wanting to be made something as workers, and they want Christ to reinforce *them*, come behind *them*, and make *them* something as His servants and in His service. **That whole system of things** [*self-actualization*] **is diametrically opposed to the truth** [*Triune-Agape*].

The truth is that **Christ shall be all**, and that we decrease that He may increase [*i.e. atomic nuclear fusion: individual atoms lose their autonomous nuclei to become one solitary nucleus*]; that **He should be the primary Personality**, and that the impact and registration of any life and any service should not be, "What a good man he was!" or "What a good woman she is!" or "What a fine worker!" but: "What a Presence of Christ! ...What an expression of Christ! ...What a reality of Christ! Are our hearts set upon God having that which is wholly of Himself? **That means "I" crucified!** No longer I, but Christ![5]

Father, Son, and Spirit live in perpetual fusion within the Nucleus of one God-Man: God in Christ; we believers are in Christ as the many-membered body

---

[5] T. Austin Sparks, (1968). *Christ in You.* First published in "A Witness and A Testimony" magazine, Mar-Apr 1968, Vol. 46-2.

of this same one new man. Recognize God's **prime directive** for the church: "Therefore **be imitators of God** [*three Self-sharers, an Us in fusion Oneness*], as beloved children [*an us regenerated with Their fuse-able DNA*]; and **walk in *Agape*** [*reciprocal sacrificial self-sharing*], just as Christ loved us and gave Himself up for us, an offering and a sacrifice to God [*e.g. the Son Jesus gives you and me, within Himself, to God*] as a **fragrant aroma**" (Eph. 5:1-2). Our Triune-Creator has long desired to smell the sweet fragrance of reciprocal *Agape* in and among Their created beings: "For we [*sacrificial self-sharers in fusion*] are **the fragrance of Christ** [*one new man*] **to God**" (2 Cor. 2:15).

The fragrance of our oneness in Christ is the *spiritual* fulfillment of the altar of incense in the *physical* Temple (2 Chron. 2:6). You and I are "holy brethren [*born of one gene-rous bloodline*], partakers of a heavenly calling [*e.g. sharers in the Son's own vocation as Priest to God and man*]" (Heb. 3:1). As members of the one body of this one Man, **Jesus' own priesthood** (ministry of gene-rosity) **is now expressed through us**: "Be of the same mind with one another according to Christ Jesus [*the mind of Christ: us thinking*], that with **one accord** you may with **one voice** glorify the God and Father of our Lord Jesus Christ [*e.g. as a fragrant aroma*]" (Rom. 15:5-6). In Revelation, John described Jesus, the "Son of Man" (Rev. 1:13), saying, "**His voice was like the sound of many waters** [*one voice comprised of many harmonious voices*]" (Rev.

1:15). Dietrich Bonhoeffer identified **unison singing** as an aspect of Christ's own priesthood expressed through us, His many-membered body:

> This is singing from the heart, singing to the Lord, singing the Word, this is **singing in unity** [*voices in fusion: one voice, a fragrant aroma*]. There is no place in the service of worship where vanity and bad taste can so intrude as in the singing.... There is the **solo voice** that goes swaggering, swelling, blaring, and tremulant from a full chest and drowns out everything else to the glory of its own fine organ [*self-worship*].... **Unison singing**, difficult as it is, is less of a musical than **a spiritual matter** [*e.g. an expression of sacrificial self-sharers in fusion*]....
>
> It is the voice of the Church that is heard in singing together. It is not you that sings [*as an individualist*], it is the Church [*one many-membered man*] that is singing, and you [*the self-sharing individual*], as a member of the Church [*corpus*], may **share in its song**. Thus all singing together that is right [*e.g. Trinity-like*] must serve to **widen our spiritual horizon** [*e.g. to see deeper and emigrate further into the*

cohabitation of our Triune-God embodied in Christ].[6]

Since the living corpus of the God-Man Jesus is *itself* the Nucleus of the kingdom, to see, enter, and participate in this cohabitation of God, we must learn how to **recognize, identify, and discern Jesus' body**. After His death and resurrection, Jesus retained His fleshly body that still bore the holes where He had been pierced by the thorns, the nails, and the spear, yet His body (*corpus*) had also been fundamentally altered. Mary Magdalene was first to discover the empty tomb but she "**did not find the body of the Lord Jesus**" (Luke 24:3). Mary "turned around and saw Jesus standing there, and **did not know that it was Jesus**...supposing Him to be the gardener" (John 20:14-16). Then, Jesus spoke her name, "Mary!" and **she recognized Him** and went to the disciples announcing, "I have seen the Lord [*God in Christ*]" (John 20:18).

That very day, Jesus caught up with two disciples on the road to Emmaus who were discussing His death and these early reports of His resurrection. Though they were walking and talking together with Jesus, **they did not recognize Him**. "When He had reclined at the table with them, He took **bread**, and breaking it, He began giving it to them [*the Self-sharing of God in Christ: three Ingredients mixed and baked by Agape into one Cake*]; then their eyes were opened and **they**

---

[6] Dietrich Bonhoeffer, *Life Together*, Harper & Row, p. 60-61.

recognized Him; and He vanished from their sight" (Luke 24:30-31). Paul helped us understand why those who knew Jesus so intimately in His previous, pre-resurrected state did not recognize Him afterward:

> [16]From now on we recognize no one according to the flesh [*as an autonomous, disjointed individual*]; even though we have known Christ according to the flesh, yet now **we know Him in this way no longer** [*e.g. as a Man in whose body you and I are not fused as "members"*]. [17]Therefore, if anyone is **in Christ** [*incorporated into the corpus; fused into the God-Man Nucleus*] he is a new creature [*lit. new creation; a member of "one new man"*]; the old things [*autonomy, individualism*] passed away; behold **new things have come** [*human beings in Trinity-like Oneness*] (2 Cor. 5:16-17).

In death and resurrection, the human body of the Son Jesus was "**glorified**" (John 13:31; Rom. 8:17), that is, His fleshly body was **perfected as the Nucleus of the fusion of the Trinity and human beings**. Now, you and I must learn to recognize, discern, and participate in this spiritual, many-membered body. Jesus said "For where two or three have gathered together in My name [*as self-sharers in fusion in the God-Man Nucleus*], I AM there in their midst" (Matt.

18:20). This reality is observed, magnified, and proclaimed when you and I, together, share the bread (body) and the cup (blood) of Christ. Paul wrote:

> [27]Therefore whoever eats the bread or drinks the cup of the Lord [*the Triune-God in Christ*] in an **unworthy manner** [*e.g. partaking for me as a self-conscious, self-indulgent individualist*], shall be guilty of the body and the blood of the Lord [*e.g. I perpetuate the relational fission which made His death necessary*]. [28]But a man must examine himself [*deny himself; forsake self-worth-ship*], and in so doing he is to eat of the bread and drink of the cup [*e.g. for the sake of the whole body, I receive strength to continue sacrificially sharing myself*]. [29]For he who eats and drinks, eats and drinks **judgment** to himself if he does not **judge** [*discern, recognize*] **the body rightly** [*e.g. partaking means I am incorporated into one, many-membered corpus: an us fused into one Nucleus*] (1 Cor. 11:27-29).

Nourishing the Body

The one, many-membered body of the one new man grows and matures from three basic sources of nourishment: 1. In the flesh and blood of Christ as Father, Son, and Spirit feed *Themselves* to us as fusion fuel; apart from **eating Jesus** together, you and I would have nothing to share with one another. 2. **Each sacrificial self-sharing member** of the body *gene-rously* feeds the other members from the bounty he himself is receiving. 3. **Each relationship** of reciprocal self-sharing (*Agape*) between individual members of the body who abide in sustained fusion with one another *gene-rates* a yield of bounty that provides nourishment for the rest of the body.

"Jesus said to them, 'Truly, truly, I say to you, **unless you eat the flesh of the Son of Man and drink His blood, you have no life in yourselves** [*e.g. to share with one another*]'" (John 6:53). Martin Luther observed that Father, Son, and Spirit are three Ingredients mixed and baked by *Agape* into **one Cake**; the Trinity feed Themselves to human beings in the flesh (bread) of the God-Man Jesus. The Triune-God is in Christ's body, and we human beings are in Christ's body. The Source of the growth and life of this many-membered body comes from sharing and eating the one Cake of God in Christ together. The prophet Isaiah foretold this:

> [6]**The Lord of hosts will prepare a lavish banquet for all peoples on this mountain** [*cohabitation of Holy, Holy, Holy; inclusive hospitality*], a banquet of aged wine [*blood*], choice pieces with marrow [*body*], and **refined aged wine** [*lit. aged upon the lees; e.g. "the divine nature" tested and perfected in the bloodline/DNA of a God-Man, made*

communicable to human beings as antidotal nourishment]. [7]And on this mountain He will swallow up the covering which is over all peoples, even **the veil** [*eclipse*] which is stretched over all nations [*Triune-God revealed in Christ in unshielded Light*]. [8]He will swallow up death [*corruption, fission decay*] for all time (Isa. 25:6-8).

Sharing this nourishment is more than simply observing communion as a religious rite or partaking in a self-conscious manner as a means of alleviating guilt by the forgiveness of my sins. Rather, celebrating the Lord's table is essentially magnifying and worth-shipping the Triune-God in Christ together and acknowledging and cherishing our place fit together in Him in such a way that causes us as one body to grow and act and mature in the sacrificial self-sharing image and fuse-able likeness of the Us of our genesis.

[16]Is not the cup of blessing which we bless a **sharing** in the blood of Christ [*one fuse-able bloodline/DNA*]? Is not the bread [*lit. one loaf*] which we break a **sharing** in the body of Christ [*fused together with Father, Son, and Spirit in one God-Man Nucleus*]? [17]Since there is **one bread** [*God in Christ: three Ingredients in one Cake*], **we who are many** [*unique, free individuals*] **are one body** [*fused individually and corporately as members of one new man*]; for **we all**

partake of the one bread [*eating Jesus: sharing in the life of three sacrificial Self-sharers*] (1 Cor. 10:16-17).

As we, together, spiritually ingest and assimilate the **flesh and blood of the God-Man Jesus** (one Cake) into ourselves as one body, we are assimilated (fused) into the oneness of the Triune-God. In this intimate, sacrificial way of inclusive hospitality, the Lord God of hosts accommodates and feeds all of us in Christ. There is certainly an individual dimension to receiving and accepting this invitation (the gospel) of God in Christ, yet only as an us in fusion oneness can you and I truly come to wholeness and abiding rest. As fellow believers, we are mixed and baked together into the one loaf of Christ by the same fuse-able, *Agape* DNA that has mixed and baked Father, Son, and Spirit into one Cake from eternity. Jesus prayed:

> [21]That they [*individual believers*] **also may be in Us**.... [22]The glory [*fuse-able DNA of Agape*] which You have given Me [*as a Man*] I have given [*made communicable*] to them, that they may all be **one** just as We [*Father, Son, Spirit*] are **one;** [23]I in them and You in Me, that they may be perfected in unity [*Trinity-like fusion*] (John 17:21-23).

In 1523, Martin Luther delivered a reformational sermon entitled, *All Become One Cake*:

You know that when a person bakes bread all the grain is thoroughly ground. Thus **each kernel becomes flour with all the others**, and thus are mixed together so that in one sack of flour the grain is so mixed and thrown together that each becomes the flour of the other [*i.e. atomic nuclear fusion: individual atoms fused into one nucleus*]. **No kernel retains its form.** Each gives to the other its flour and **each loses its own body** [*i.e. autonomous nucleus*]. Thus many small kernels of grain become **one loaf of bread** [*Nucleus of Christ's many-membered body*], just as in the same way when one makes **wine**, each grape mixes its juice with that of the others and each forsakes its form [*e.g. individualism*]. **From all comes one drink.**

Thus it should also be with us. **I give myself for the common good** and serve you, and you make use of what is mine of which you are in need [*Agape: reciprocal self-sharing*]. Thus I AM your food...I AM your bread...you partake of me, and I in turn partake of you.... Thus **God places us in the fellowship of Christ and all His chosen** [*God feeds Himself to us through one another*]; there we have a great consolation [*a shared nest of relational rest*] where we **forsake ourselves** [*reciprocating the extreme self-forsaking Love of our Triune-God*].

This we do not understand [*eclipsed in eros rationale*], and if we likewise often hear and understand it, we do not believe it. And so **we retreat ever more and experience no fruit** or improvement [*e.g. in unbelief and self-preservation, I retreat into my own locked garden*]…You must see how **you are beginning another life** [*as a member of the body of one new man*], that you are disgusted with your former life [*the old self: corrupted by individualism, self-worth-ship*], and be satisfied with that.[7]

Reflecting on our Triune-Creator's brilliant design and formation of this one new man, I think about how the secular world cannot stop chasing all sorts of philosophical rabbit trails and engaging in endless, futile speculations attempting to solve the mystery: **Who are we as human beings?** What are we supposed to do and to be? Why are we here? Where did we come from? How do we discover the meaning and purpose of our existence? Comprehensive and rational answers beyond man's wildest imagination lie hidden in plain sight in the Scriptures, but in our *de-gene-*

---

[7] Martin Luther, *All Become One Cake*; sermon given Maundy Thursday 1523, translated by Matthew Harrison.

rate condition we are simply incapable of seeing them because we invariably begin our search with godless presuppositions of *eros* individualism and self-worthship. We seek answers in and from ourselves: "Men suppress the truth [*Triune-Agape*] in unrighteousness [*eros individualism*]" (Rom. 1:18). The very questions we ask are self-referential; therefore, the answers lie just out of reach!

As the Son of God, Jesus is the Nucleus of the Triune-God; as **the Son of Man**, Jesus is the Nucleus of *all* humanity. Oswald Chambers observed, "Jesus Christ is not an individual iota of a man; He is **the whole of the human race centered before God in one Person**: He is God and Man in **one** [*Nucleus of the Trinity and man*].[8] Paul wrote, God **"chose us in Him** [*as members of the corpus of Christ*] **before the foundation of the world**" (Eph. 1:4). Outside of the one new man who is the Son of Man it is impossible for human beings to find the meaning and purpose in their existence: "For we [*human beings*] are His workmanship, **created in Christ Jesus** [*as members of His body*] **for good works**, which God prepared beforehand [*before creation*] so that we would walk in them" (Eph. 2:10). Further, apart from incorporation into the corpus of Christ, it is impossible for an individual's uniqueness and full potential (*in-gen-uity*) to be discovered and released.

As the Nucleus of mankind, Jesus is painfully

---

[8] Chambers, Oswald (2000), *The Complete Works of Oswald Chambers*. Discovery House Publishers, Grand Rapids, MI, p. 22.

aware *within* Himself of the de-gene-rate nature of individualism in human beings and our condition in fission from God and one another. Through David, the eternal Son spoke in prophetic detail of His crucifixion including the statement, "**all my bones are out of joint**" (Ps. 22:14). In relational alienation, enmity, and fission from one another, you and I are the bones of Jesus' very Own body, which are out of joint—a condition of **acute suffering** that He experiences in the most *personal* way. Dwelling in fullness in the body of the Son Jesus as a Man, Father and Spirit came into perfect alignment in Him over the course of 33 years. At the Cross, however, these three Self-sharers *Themselves* bore the agony of our **relational disjointing** (fission) so that we might be brought into proper **relational alignment** (fusion) as functional members in His one body. See how Paul sacrificially gave himself to Jesus as a self-sharer in His body:

> [17]In Him [*Christ, the God-Man Nucleus*] all things hold together. [18]He is also **the head of the body, the church** [*unique individuals incorporated into the corpus of God in Christ*].... [22]He has now **reconciled you** [*to God and one another*] **in His fleshly body through death** [*embracing, overcoming, and defeating relational fission*].... [24]Now I [*Paul, a man in Christ*] rejoice in my sufferings for your sake [*as a*

sacrificial self-sharer], and in my flesh **I do my share on behalf of His body**, which is the church, in filling up what is lacking in Christ's afflictions (Col. 1:17-24).

To illustrate how the nourishment, which our Triune-God provides, is conducted **through each individual member** fused into His body, Jesus provided another analogy:

> [4]As the branch cannot bear fruit of itself unless it abides in the vine, so neither can you unless you abide in Me [*God in Christ*]. [5]I AM the vine, you are the branches; he who abides in Me, and I in him [*in Trinity-like fusion*] bears much fruit [*superabundant gene-rosity*], for apart from Me you can do nothing [*e.g. you have nothing to share*] (John 15:4-5).

Now, let's take this a step further and see how God works to nourish the whole man **through each relationship** of reciprocal gene-rosity that is cultivated between individual members of the body like you and me:

> Christ is the head [*Nucleus and Source*], from whom the entire [*many-membered*] body, **being supplied and held together by the joints and ligaments** [*lit. bonds; fusion relationships between its self-sharing*

members], grows with a growth [*re-gene-ration*] which is from God [*e.g. in the image and likeness of three Self-sharers who are one God*] (Col. 2:19).

As "a man in Christ" (2 Cor. 12:2), Paul participated as a sacrificial self-sharer in the one body, cultivating relationships and cherishing and nourishing the one new man at great personal cost. Therefore, from *within* the body, Paul developed a profound, working knowledge of God's design and blueprints for this living, functioning, many-membered corpus:

> [13]Until we [*together*] **attain to the unity of the faith** [*perfected in fusion oneness in Christ even as the Trinity is one in Christ*], and of the true knowledge of the Son of God [*the God-Man Nucleus*], to **a mature man** [*one functional many-membered body: sharing one nature, name, mind, purpose in Trinity-likeness*], to the measure of the stature which belongs to **the fullness of Christ** [*we, as a created us conformed to the image of the uncreated Us Gen 1:26*]. [15]...we [*together*] are to **grow up in all aspects into Him** [*e.g. perfected in unity John 17:23*] who is the head, even Christ, [16]from whom the whole body, **being fitted and held together by what every joint** [*relationship of reciprocal gene-rosity*]

supplies, according to the proper working [*sacrificial self-sharing*] of **each individual part**, causes the **growth** [*nourishment, wholeness*] of the body for the building up of itself in *Agape* (Eph. 4:13-16).

Forbearing, forgiving, and sustaining other members to whom I am jointed certainly requires me to make personal sacrifices, yet my motivation in paying these costs may not necessarily be for the sake of Jesus' body. I may maintain peace with others **for my own sake**: to neutralize confrontation, prevent being disturbed, and avoid rocking the boat in which I find myself sitting too far from shore to disembark. Though this form of peace-keeping can be helpful, it is a far more powerful *Agape* motivation to sacrificially absorb the traumatic jolts, shocks, and stresses of being jointed to others and maintain relational alignment with them **for Jesus' sake**: for the sake of His own body, because I consciously and intentionally "seek first His" (Matt. 6:33).

As individual members of Jesus' body, when you and I are functioning properly in the relational dynamic of reciprocal sacrificial self-sharing, Jesus feels *within Himself* unencumbered mobility, dexterity, and agility in the "joints and ligaments" of His own body. Dietrich Bonhoeffer described the practical implications of this one, interdependent, many-membered body:

> Every act of **self-control** of the Christian [*denying self to share self*] is a service to

the fellowship. On the other hand, there is no **sin** [*manifestation of self-worth-ship*] in thought, word, or deed, no matter how personal or secret, that does not **inflict injury** upon the whole fellowship. **An element of sickness** [*eros individualism*] gets into the body; perhaps nobody knows where it comes from or in what member it has lodged, but **the body is infected**…. We are members of a body, not only when we choose to be, but in our whole existence. Every member serves the whole body, either to its **health** or to its **destruction**. This is no mere theory; it is a spiritual reality.[9]

King David in Dress Rehearsal

The kingdom [*cohabitation*] of God is entirely facilitated within the King, within one Man—"God in Christ" (Col. 2:9; 2 Cor. 5:19; Eph. 4:32; see also Ezek. 1:26-28). The life of David was an elaborate, sovereign dress rehearsal of the life of Christ. Through the eternal Spirit Who fell repeatedly and mightily on David, the eternal Son spoke words through David that He Himself would speak thousands of years later as the incarnate God-Man Jesus, including "My God, My God, why have You forsaken Me" (Ps.

---

[9] Dietrich Bonhoeffer, (1954). *Life Together*, Harper & Row Publishers, New York. p. 89.

22:1; Matt. 27:46). The **Star of David** symbolized his expectant faith, hope, and *Agape* for the coming of the Messiah—**the Nucleus of the fusion of God and man**—whose birth was indicated by a **star**. The angel Gabriel announced to Mary, "The Lord God will give Him [*Jesus*] the throne of His father David" (Luke 1:32). David and the tribes of Israel served as an imperfect, yet true prophetic model of Christ Jesus and us:

> [12]For day by day, men came to David [*the man God chose to facilitate His cohabitation of self-sharers*] to help him [*e.g. to seek first His*], until there was a great army, like the army of God [*multitudes of individuals, families, and tribes in fusion*]. [33]…they helped David with an undivided heart [*lit. not of double heart*]. [38]…All these, being men of war who could draw up in battle formation, came to Hebron with **a perfect heart** [*e.g. unrestrained affection: Agape without hypocrisy; Trinity-likeness*] to make David king over all Israel; and all the rest of Israel were also of one mind to make David king [*the nucleus of the kingdom*]."
> (1 Chron. 12:22-38).

Truly, there is nothing stronger than **the heart of a volunteer**—the willing spirit, soul, and body of a sacrificial self-sharer! In a prophetic psalm, David sang, "**Your people will volunteer freely** [*lit. will be* *freewill offerings*] **in the day of Your** [*fusion*] **power**; in holy array [*self-sharers standing in military formation*], from the womb of the dawn [*e.g. the resurrection of Christ*], Your youth [*re-gene-rated children*] are to You as the dew [*e.g. life-source in the barren wilderness of Worthless' world*]" (Ps. 110:3). Through Zephaniah, the Lord added, "I will give to the people purified lips [*purged from self-referential, self-promoting speech*], that all of them may call upon the name of the Lord, **to serve Him shoulder to shoulder**" (Zeph. 3:9).

Later in King David's reign, his son Absalom was consumed by self-worth-ship and became a treacherous individualist with a deep aversion to sharing and a powerful instinct and ambition to exalt himself:

> [4]Absalom would say, "Oh that one would **appoint me judge** in the land, then every man who has any suit or cause could come to me and **I would give him justice**." [5]And when a man came near to prostrate himself before him, he would put out his hand and take hold of him and kiss him. [6]In this manner Absalom dealt with all Israel who came to the king for judgment; so **Absalom stole away the hearts of the men of Israel** (2 Sam. 15:4-6).

At an opportune time, Absalom usurped the throne, forced David to flee Jerusalem into exile, and "Absalom went in to his father's concubines in the sight of all Israel" (2 Sam. 16:22). However, this wayward son ran his course in upward descent and was ultimately dethroned. Cut off from his own army and fleeing from David's mighty volunteers, "his head caught fast in the thick branches of an oak tree so he was **left hanging between heaven and earth** while the mule that was under him kept going." Suspended there, Absalom met the **Triune-God of justice**: "Joab [*the commander of David's men*]…took **three spears** in his hand and thrust them through the heart of Absalom" (2 Sam. 18:9-14). Afterward, the Lord provided a fresh opportunity to **renew Zion**, the prophetic model of Christ's kingdom of sacrificial self-sharers who volunteer freely:

> King David sent Zadok and Abiathar the priests, saying, "Speak to the elders of Judah [*David's own tribe*], saying, '**Why are you the last to bring the king back to his house**, since the word of all Israel [*the invitation of the other 11 tribes*] has come to the king, even to his house? **You are my brothers; you are my bone and my flesh.** Why then should you be the last to bring back the king?'" Thus David turned the hearts [*affectionate allegiance*] of all the men of Judah as **one man** so that they sent word to the king, saying, "Return, you and all your servants" (2 Sam. 19:11-14).

Recognizing mature *Agape* as sacrificial self-sharing Love and gaining a basic knowledge of the blueprints of the cohabitation of the Trinity and individual human beings in the Nucleus (*corpus*) of the God-Man Jesus has laid a foundation of understanding that will enable us to **see law and justice from God's perspective**.

In the next volume, *God Magnified Part 10: Observing Justice and Equality*, we will magnify "**the Lord is a God of justice**" (Isa. 30:18) and discover how our Triune-God preserves the freedom and equality of individuals in the cohabitation of the kingdom according to the law of *Agape*.

God Magnified Series

Part 1: Discovering the "Us" in Oneness

A journey of progressive magnification of the worth-ship of God by meditating on five of the fourteen "God is" statements in Scripture. These statements are like porch pillars of the eternal dwelling place that the Trinity share in perpetual fusion Oneness in *Agape*. The Triune-God intentionally left Their spiritual fingerprint in the powersource of the natural universe—atomic nuclear fusion—"God is a sun."

Part 2: Exploring the Dwelling Place

Our journey continues around the porch pillars of the eternal dwelling place of Light in which the Father, Son, and Spirit indwell One Another in fusion Oneness. Eric leads us through a clear understanding of "God is Light" and "God is a sun and shield" explaining the vortex of the Trinity and how we are called to be sharers of their holiness and mature children of Light.

Part 3: Revealing the Secret of the Mystery

This volume focuses on Pillar 8, "God in Christ," where we discover the secret mystery of our participation in the dynamic of the kingdom—the fusion of the Triune-God and regenerated sons and daughters dwelling together in the God-Man Jesus.

Part 4: Awakening to Spiritual Reality

This volume focuses on Pillar 9, "God is Spirit," where we discover how Father, Son, and Spirit fuse into One Another as a whirlwind. The Triune-Spirit created individual human beings as a tri-unity—spirit, soul, and body. We will learn how as free individuals we are fused by *Agape* into the Triune-Spirit.

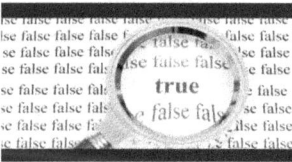

Part 5: Discerning "The Truth"

This volume focuses on Pillar 10, "God is true," revealing a deeper understanding of the divine nature of *Agape*—the "true" Love by which Father, Son, and Spirit abide in perpetual fusion as one God. We will discover how truth is in Jesus and how we by His grace becomes sharers of that truth. By carefully examining and receiving this truth, which the Triune-God desires to plant, cultivate, and mature within us, we are made capable of participating in a relationship of reciprocal generosity with Father, Son, Spirit and one another—the kingdom of God.

Part 6: Appraising the Most High

"O magnify the Lord with me!" (Ps. 34:3). One effective way to closely examine and worth-ship God is to meditate on what the Scriptures specifically testify that "God is." As the Holy Spirit progressively opens the *God is* statements of the Bible to us, we discover the fusion of the Trinity. In this sixth volume, we continue investigating "God is true" (John 3:33) to discover why Father, Son, and Spirit, together are "the Most High God" (Ps. 78:35; Heb. 7:1). The Scriptures consistently use economic terms to describe how these three Eternals add to and exalt One Another by sacrifical Self-giving. The economy of the kingdom functions by giving and receiving in order to give again, which yields superabundant bounty. When we "exchanged the truth of God for the lie" (Rom. 1:25), we fell out of the abundant life of the Most High and bought into the corrupt economy of the world that operates by buying and selling one another for self-indulgence, which precipitates famine.

Part 7: Surveying the Economy of the Kingdom

"O magnify the Lord with me!" (Ps. 34:3). One effective way to closely examine and worth-ship God is to meditate on what the Scriptures specifically testify that "God is." As the Holy Spirit progressively opens the *God is* statements of the Bible to us, we discover the fusion of the Trinity. In this seventh volume, we continue investigating "God is True" (John 3:33). The Scriptures consistently use economic terms to describe how these three Eternals add to and exalt One Another by sacrifical Self-giving. The economy of the kingdom functions by giving and receiving in order to give again, which yields superabundant bounty. When we "exchanged the truth of God for the lie" (Romans 1:25), we fell out of the abundant life of the Most High and bought into the corrupt economy of the world, which operates by buying and selling one another and precipitates famine. Jesus came to lift us in Himself and mentor us in Kingdom economics as sons of the Most High.

Part 8: Unveiling Three Sacrificial Self-Sharers

"O magnify the Lord with me" (Ps. 34:3). One effective way to closely examine and worth-ship God is to meditate on what the Scriptures specifically testify that "God is." As the Holy Spirit opens the God is statements of the Bible to us, we discover the fusion of the Trinity. In this eighth volume, "Unveiling Three Sacrificial Self-sharers," we will see: 1. how Father, Son, and Spirit share all things with One Another; 2. how all the fullness of these things were shared with the Son Jesus as a Man; and 3. how, in this God-Man, the Triune-God share all things with us human beings who have bought into Him by faith stated in 1 Cor. 3:22-23, "...all things belong to you, and you belong to Christ, and Christ belongs to God." The kingdom of God is a cohabitation of individuals who are "one" in Agape–sacrificial, self-sharing Love. Father, Son, and Spirit steward this one shared estate on behalf of One Another and on our behalf as "children of God...heirs of God and fellow heirs with Christ" (Rom. 8:17).

LIFECHANGERS®

P.O. Box 3709 ❖ Cookeville, TN 38502
931.520.3730 ❖ lc@lifechangers.org

www.ingramcontent.com/pod-product-compliance
Lightning Source LLC
Chambersburg PA
CBHW071829020426
42331CB00007B/1661